Three years ago Debby Wood and her family packed up all their earthly belongings and joined a flock of southbound snowbirds on a one-way flight to Florida.

Can a harried housewife from the North give up her beloved snow and the four seasons cold turkey? Can she learn to love Florida, with all its lizards and lovebugs, sandburs and sunburn, mildew and mosquitoes?

Ever since she arrived, Debby has been entertaining fellow Floridians with her family's escapades through her warm and witty column in the Lee County Shopper.

Now, for the first time, some of the best and funniest of her works are gathered together in a collection guaranteed to bring back memories of love and laughter.

Library of Congress Catalog Card Number 80-69857

International Standard Book Number 0-89305-032-6

Printed and bound in Florida, U.S.A.
Anna Publishing, Inc., Winter Park, Florida

Fifth Printing

"Oh, God, not another beautiful day!"

By Debby Wood

To Beth and Andrea

who fill my days
with love and laughter

1

Welcome to love bug land

"We're in Florida and we thought we'd stop by!"

What in the world has happened to me?

In the short time I have lived in Florida I somehow have changed from a harried but happy housewife to a combination innkeeper-travel agent!

It all started even before we got here. One of my friends asked me to find a condominium where she and "anywhere from one to three others" could spend "up to three months, sometime during the winter."

How much rent did they want to pay? Where did they want to stay? When would they like to begin their vacation?

They had no idea. "Just find something for us," she said with a smile.

I spent weeks carting my children all over Lee County looking at apartments, and finally found four that would have been ideal. She chose one, via long-distance, and we paid the deposit.

Two days later she changed her mind. She and one other woman would come down for just two weeks in March instead!

I smiled, muttered a few words under my breath and then started looking for March vacancies.

One of my relatives arrived around Thanksgiving for what we expected would be a week-long visit. No sooner had she stepped off the plane than she decided it was too beautiful for such a brief visit. She'd just have to stay another week or so.

It was then that I began to realize that the visits that up North lasted overnight or at the most for a long weekend,

8

down here range anywhere from three days to three months. But then, I guess everything grows in Florida.

On Dec. 14 I got a call from a casual acquaintance in Western New York. She and her family had planned to spend Christmas in a rented condo on the east coast but something had gone wrong and it was no longer available.

Could I possibly look around and see if I could find them a place before they arrived on the 20th?

Sure, says I. Now just how many will there be in your party?

"Probably around 12."

Good Heavens!

But it was company that helped me overcome my homesickness over the holidays. My sister and her family were down for Christmas and on Jan. 1 some dear old friends arrived. They spent three of the coldest, wettest days I've ever seen here just trying to find the sun. They never did.

I'm getting to the point where I feel embarrassed, and somewhat guilty, when the weather is lousy for my visitors.

Old college friends just left after a terrific five-day stay and, believe it or not, we are already booked up for the entire month of March!

Do I hate it? Not on your life.

I'm really getting the hang of it. I bet I can change sheets faster than a Holiday Inn chambermaid and I'll bet I know almost as much about Edison's house as the old gent did himself. The Waltzing Waters are dancing in my sleep and I'm practically on a first name basis with half the realtors and motel owners in Lee County.

Snowbirds are the ones with the beautiful tans

I've learned that weather plays an important role in life in Florida. I've noticed that the weather up north is of more interest to us down south than it is to those up north who are actually experiencing it. The local weathermen seem to take a perverse delight in reporting snowstorms around the country.

My father loves to start each day with the statement, "Oh, God, not another beautiful day!" Then he breaks into a big grin.

I'll never forget my first experience with "cold" weather in Florida. We had just arrived, and we went to a high school football game to see my brother play. The temperature must have been about 60 degrees, and everyone in the bleachers was wearing coats, sweaters, caps, gloves and scarfs. Not my family. We were dressed in shorts and T-shirts, enjoying the warm Florida climate! To us, 60 degrees was like a heat wave.

How quickly things change. Now, when the thermometer dips below 70, I start rooting through the drawers looking for the sweaters and the warm coats. During one recent "cold snap" my daughter asked if it would snow.

This strange phenomenon of being cold on a warm day brings varying reactions from different people. Friends and neighbors nod their heads knowingly and mumble something about the blood thinning out in the hot climate. But my friends up north just laugh and say I've had a heatstroke! I always have the last laugh, however. All I do is ask them what the temperature is up north.

My first few years in Florida have been a learning experience. I've learned:

• Always ride your bicycle with your mouth closed. It prevents a lot of surprises.

• It's easy to tell which people are snowbirds. They're the ones with the suntans.

• You can learn to live with bugs. Well, almost.

• You can't live in the Florida sunshine without at least one aloe plant in your garden.

• You can't cool your swimming pool in the summer by throwing trays of ice cubes in the water.

• You can't afford to heat your pool in the winter, no matter who comes to visit.

• Crabs are fun to catch and fun to eat, but I'm not sure they're worth the trouble to clean.

• You must keep your house clean and neat at all times because the next phone call may be an unexpected visitor from the north.

• There are a lot of great trips you can take in Florida -- in the summer, after the rates go down!

• Love bugs are bugs you hate.

• Sand spurs spur anger in even the most gentle person.

• Fire ants will eventually take over the world. They've already taken over my yard.

• The mosquito is Public Enemy Number 1. And Number 2, and Number 3, and ...

• The slowest drivers always drive in the center lane, except when they are making a left turn.

• Once you open a bag of potato chips in this humidity, you might just as well eat them all.

• Deodorant commercials take on a new meaning when you live in Florida.

Bug off, buster, the love bugs have arrived

June seems to be the most popular month for brides and grooms but May is definitely the honeymoon month for love bugs.

From the look of things I'd say most of the love bugs from throughout the country have decided to honeymoon in Florida this year. Unfortunately my car has put an abrupt end to the nuptials of several hundred of the pesky critters, and the season is only half over.

Love bugs, for those of you who haven't been outside of your house for the past few weeks, are those little black bugs who swarm up from the ground in pairs and smash into the hood of your car. The bugs are actually mating in mid-air -- an experience they are unlikely to forget if they don't happen to be in front of a car. But a lot of them seem to end up mating in front of my windshield, and I don't mind telling you it's a sight I don't particularly enjoy.

They tell me that you should wash the dead lovebugs off

the hood of your car because the bugs can ruin the paint finish. I really don't have that problem. Our car is in such bad shape already that a few more spots don't readily show up.

I have noticed a lot of drivers have attached nets or screens over the hood and grill of the car. It looks pretty silly, but I guess it is a good way to protect the car.

A friend of mine suggested I put a coat of petroleum jelly or baby oil on the hood of the car, but I just can't convince myself to take such a drastic step. I'm sure the neighbors would start talking!

But enough of my problems. What about the lovebugs? They surely have a sad tale to tell. To get some of the answers about the burning issues of the month, I went to Felix Amour, world-renowned specialist on love bugs and professor of bugology at the University of Fort Myers.

"Dr. Amour," I asked, "why did you start studying the mating habits of love bugs?"

"It all began about 15 years ago during a vacation in the South," he said with a smile. "I was driving down the Florida Turnpike when my white car suddenly was covered with black polka dots."

"I screeched to a halt, got out of the car and went over to the hood to inspect the damage. Just then a bug that had been flattened out against the headlight lifted her little head, wiped a drop of sweat from her forehead, said 'Is that all there is?' and died on the spot."

"From that moment I knew it was my destiny in life to uncover the mystery of love bugs, and I have devoted every spare minute to that task," he said.

Why do they make love on the highways, I asked.

"The answer is simple," he said. "They can't find beds that tiny. And even if they could find them, they couldn't afford to buy them. Times being what they are, most love bugs are living on love, not money."

"I've heard, Dr. Amour, that the love bugs are attracted by exhaust fumes on the highways," I said.

"That's nonsense," he shouted. "Just a silly rumor being spread by the big oil companies. They're trying to create a demand for the new gas-scented perfume they plan to market next summer. They think they can fool the public into believing that exhaust fumes are an aphrodisiac.''

I asked Dr. Amour how many love bugs survive the mating season.

"About 30 percent, I guess. Most people think the rest are highway victims, but actually only about 10 percent become hood ornaments. The vast majority are trampled by cows.''

Why cows, I asked.

"Well, love bugs spend their formative years in grassy fields, constantly searching for a mate. Many spend years in the grass, looking for love. They only start flying in desperation, after they have given up all hope of splendor in the grass. And we all know that cows tramp around in those same grassy fields. Cows cause an untimely end for 40 percent of all love bugs.''

I asked him why so many love bugs ended up in Florida.

"They started in Niagara Falls," he said, "but the winters were too harsh. So they headed south. No bug in his right mind would spend the winter near Buffalo!''

"I'm always amazed," I said, "that the love bugs are able to stay attached as they fly around. How do they do it?''

"Ah," Dr. Amour said with a sly grin, "that took me years to find out. For a long while I thought they were magnetic, and then I explored the possibility that they secreted some type of glue.''

"But about four years ago I discovered that all love bugs, when they reach five years of age, are enrolled in acrobatic school. They learn tumbling, gymnastics, and they even work out on the parallel bars. It takes months of practice before they are sent out on the highway to make love.''

At that point Dr. Amour took a little plastic box from his coat pocket and showed me six pair of love bugs. I noticed one of the love bugs had some white specks on his back and I looked through a magnifier to see what it was.

Imagine my surprise when I read the words **MAKE LOVE, NOT WAR** painted on a tiny bumper sticker on his back.

I chuckled out loud and the startled love bug looked up with a sneer and said "Bug off, buster. This ain't no X-rated movie."

If you don't want to crab, keep your trap shut

Fellow Floridians, tell me please, how in the world do you catch a crab?

When I was contemplating moving here, I would envision myself sitting out on my patio, basking in the sun and feasting on mounds of crabmeat I had just caught in my own little trap.

Ah, it would be heaven.

As soon as I got here I did some extensive investigating and finally purchased what I was told was the Cadillac of crab traps. "Believe me," said the man, "you put this in your canal and you'll probably catch an average of six crabs a day."

Off I ran to the grocery store and bought a nice frying chicken to use as bait -- nothing but the best for my crabs. I figured if the menu looked good, they'd all want to come to my trap for dinner.

I dashed home and pulled my oldest daughter down to the dock to watch the big event. We baited the trap as told, threw it into the canal and waited to catch our dinner. Nothing.

After staring at it for about an hour, I decided to go back in the house and fix lunch. Maybe, I thought, they liked to dine alone. About an hour later I ran out to check -- nothing. "Oh well, there's plenty of time until dinner."

My husband came home from work about 5:30 p.m., hungry as a bear and as anxious as I was for our long-awaited feast. We went down to the trap. Nothing.

As we sat eating our peanut butter and jelly sandwiches that night, we theorized that perhaps crabs just don't spot the traps right away and that maybe it takes a while for the word to spread in the crab world that my delicious new restaurant was now open and awaiting some business.

Nothing.

Well, folks, months later I'm still waiting for my big crab dinner.

One day I caught two -- one large and one very small. Yea, I thought, the word has finally gotten around. Anticipating great things, I generously tossed the small one back into the canal and cooked and kept the big one to add to all the rest I was sure would follow. Nothing.

I tried using cut up fish for bait but it smelled so bad after two or three days that I threw it out and went back to chicken.

The only thing I seem to be able to catch is some hideously ugly fish that always eat my bait and then get stuck in the trap.

Well, several weeks later I caught Trudy.

Trudy is a small but nasty little crab that wandered into my trap and my life about four weeks ago. She must be a loner because she didn't bring any of her friends with her.

I was going to let her go, too, but after the last time I decided against it. Nope. This time I was going to put Trudy to work for me.

I'd give her room and board in my wonderful trap and in exchange she could entice all her friends who happened to pass by to stop in for a bite to eat. Meanwhile, Trudy herself could grow and grow until she, too, got big enough to join us at the table. I look upon this as my own little 4-H project.

Well, as I said before, Trudy must not be too popular. She hasn't had one visitor yet and I'm still not getting anywhere. There must be some tricks that I just don't know.

So if anyone has any ideas, let me know. I'm getting mighty hungry and Trudy'd love the company!

This story is a bare-faced lie, but just grin and bear it

You probably have already heard about the bear that was seen roaming through South Fort Myers recently. All the radio and television stations and the newspapers had stories about the bear, which was last seen heading toward the hills, wherever they are.

I first heard about the bear while I was watching television. A bulletin interrupted the movie I was watching. It warned that a dangerous bear was seen roaming around the Colonial Boulevard area and viewers were urged to stay inside their homes.

What a story, I thought, the old reporter's blood stirring through my veins. "This is something I've got to see for myself," I told my husband as I grabbed a notebook and headed through the door.

The result, I'm proud to say, is something of a journalistic coup. Better than Watergate, better than Big Foot, even better than Clifford Irving's story about Howard Hughes. Debby Wood, your own Lee County Shopper editor, got an exclusive interview with the elusive bear.

When I arrived at the scene, the policeman only laughed as I asked to talk with the bear.

"Lady, we haven't seen hide nor hair of the bear. All I know is that some folks around here claim they spotted a bear and chased it out of their neighborhood. I'd go home, if I were you," he said.

Undaunted, I searched for tracks, for hair, for any clues. Suddenly I had a hunch. Where would a bear head for? Why, the Bee Factory, of course.

Sure enough, I drove down U.S. 41 and got to the Bee Factory just as the bear was squeezing in the back door.

"Hey," I yelled, "how about an interview?"

The bear looked up, frowned and said "Who are you? Barbara Walters?"

I assured him I was just a cub reporter looking for the bare facts, and he seemed to relax. "I don't want you to

16

make a liar out of me. I have to be careful who I talk to," he said.

I asked him about his escapades earlier in the evening, when he barely had escaped with his life.

"I make this trip every year at this time," the bear said. "You see, there is this short period between when the winter tourists leave and the summer tourists arrive. That's when I come down to the Bee Factory to get enough honey to last the rest of the year."

I asked him why he only makes the trip once a year.

"Well, it's pretty hard to bear. The roads are crowded when the tourists are here, and with more tourists in the area there's more chance of someone spotting me. Besides, I don't want to be the one to scare the tourists away. They leave lots of bread here when they go back up north," he said.

I asked the bear how he was spotted this trip.

"As I was heading south, I passed the tennis courts. Then I headed over to the school to see if any children wanted to come out and play. You see, most of my friends went north for the summer, so I've been sort of lonely lately. But the school was empty, so I lumbered out of there," the bear said.

"I finally spotted some people and I ran up to them to play, but they all started running and screaming. The next thing I knew, there were people everywhere. Ladies in nighties were gathering on the street corner, dogs started barking, blue and white cars with pretty flashing lights were converging from every angle, and men bearing arms started charging at me. When I heard one man yell 'I'll get that critter with my bare hands,' I decided it was time to make a beeline out of there."

But how did you get away, I asked.

"I hid in an empty garage until things calmed down, and then I grabbed some clothes off a clothes line, put them on and walked right past the police. In the old days when crewcuts were so popular, I just couldn't have done that," he said.

"The rest of the trip was easy. Everyone was looking for a black bear, not a harried housewife. Hardly anyone gave

17

me a second glance. No one even noticed that I was bare foot," he said.

I asked him why he came all the way down to the Bee Factory to get his honey.

"It's hard for me to find food around here anymore. A lot of beehives have been replaced by bowling alleys and boutiques. The last time I went down to the river to catch fish for supper, I nearly got speared by a spear gun. And I don't get food stamps, so I can't go to Publix or Winn Dixie. Things just aren't like they used to be," he said.

"Bear up," I told him. "By the way, where do you live?"

"I've got a little place near the Rangoon Supper Club. Not very big, but it's bearable. Most of my relatives have moved east, but I like this area. I'm bullish on Lee County.

"Bear a hand here," he said as he reached into a hive and brought out some honey. "I've got to be careful. These bees are unbearable. The last time I barely escaped with my life."

I told him he was just going to have to grin and bear it, and thanked him for the interview. As I got in my car, I noticed the bear running north with a swarm of bees bearing down on his back side. The last words I heard were "Buzz off!"

Hurricane David
nearly ended in divorce

Hurricane David nearly caused a divorce at our house last year.

Had David procrastinated two more days before his unwelcome visit to South Florida, I would have been ready for a nervous breakdown. Either that or the divorce courts!

As David inched his way slowly and erratically across the hurricane chart pasted on our refrigerator, the tensions would build along with it. Our emotions -- more specifically my emotions -- seemed to see-saw back and forth between utter nonchalance and total panic.

Let me quickly point out that I'm a transplanted "Yankee" with no experience whatsoever with hurricanes. The closest I'd ever come to a hurricane was on NBC news. None of those "killer" blizzards up north had prepared me for anything like a hurricane.

I first began to worry about David when he was a little tropical depression out in the middle of nowhere. For some strange reason I had this feeling that David and I were destined to meet someday soon.

When David turned into a hurricane, I carefully put a red dot on my hurricane charting map. The map had been hanging up for three months without so much as a single mark, but something inside me told me to start charting this storm.

My husband laughed and teased me, pointing out that the storm was as far away from Fort Myers as Maine was. But I wasn't alone. A friend of mine had her provisions packed and evacuation route all mapped out and I didn't know which way to turn.

By the time it looked like David might possibly decide to take his vacation in Fort Myers, I began to get really concerned. My friend had already talked it over with her family and had come up with two plans, depending on which way David went.

My husband, on the other hand, didn't even want to discuss it. Depsite the fact that we live on a canal just two blocks from the river, six feet above water level, he could foresee no danger at all.

I was fit to be tied. Here I was, worrying about how to get all the furniture in our house as close to the ceiling as possible and all he could think about was cleaning the pool.

"Forget the pool," I screamed, near tears. "In two days it'll be as muddy as the canal. What's the sense in cleaning it now?"

As David meandered across our refrigerator during the next few days, I kept track of its direction with each news broadcast. If it went north a fraction of an inch, my spirits would soar. But every time it went west a degree, I would put a few more things in the suitcases that were by now scattered throughout the house.

What do you take with you? The first thing I packed was the photographs we have collected during the past 11 years. That was good for one suitcase alone.

I decided the insurance would cover my earthly possessions like the silver and china, but one particular porcelain dish was irreplaceable, so I wrapped it in towels and put it in another suitcase.

Then came the clothes. If we left, should we take clothes for the north or clothes for the south? I decided to make reservations in Orlando, just in case David took the southern route to the Gulf.

When my husband got home from work one day and saw all of my preparations, he exploded. "How can you go anywhere when you don't know where David is going?" he said.

I just can't understand why he couldn't understand.

The next day, though, forecasters predicted that the hurricane would head toward south Florida. That's when my friends decided to board a plane and take a three-day vacation up north. I thought it was a pretty smart idea, but my husband wouldn't go for it.

He did make one concession, though. We moved all the plants and patio furniture into the garage. And we covered the boat and tied it to the dock more securely.

That's when I realized that the female in our society always plays the heavy in these kinds of situations.

"Let's slide the heavy planter closer to the house so it won't blow into the pool?" I said. And my husband would roll his eyes toward the sky and grudgingly oblige.

"Why don't we put down the hurricane shutters on the windows, just to be safe," I said. And my husband would mutter something like "If it would make you happy" and then he'd hammer away at the shutters, cursing my suggestions.

I noticed the same thing happened with other friends and relatives here. The men seemed to blame the necessity of preparing for the hurricane, even the very existence of the hurricane, on women. As if it were our fault that the hurricanes threaten the home. Maybe that's why the storms were given women's names for so long.

When David decided to tour the east coast of Florida instead of this area, the tension in our house seemed to disappear. Well, almost. There was a little problem when we had to carry all those plants and patio furniture back outside and take off the shutters. I could see my husband's mind thinking "If it weren't for her crazy ideas, we wouldn't have to do all this work."

But as we sat in our own home Sunday night watching the television coverage of all those people in Miami evacuating from their homes, I took some comfort in the knowledge that the hurricane that caused it all was named David instead of Debby.

You're in trouble when your ship comes in

"But it's the boat of my dreams!"

Warning: The International Miami Boat Show can be hazardous to your bank account!

It makes no difference if you love boats or hate them, get seasick on the water, have two boats already or swore you'd never have another. Once you're bitten by the boat bug, you just know it's going to be fatal.

If you're felled by the bug and you buy a boat, the symptoms immediately disappear and are replaced by a heavenly euphoria.

But if you're one of those strong-willed people who somehow survive, be prepared to fight off a bout of depression.

No matter how big or beautiful your present boat is, there are yachts at the boat show that make yours look sick. And for those who have never felt any real attraction toward boating before there are the cutest, most unusual and most attractive little numbers you have ever seen.

Take me for example.

When my brother asked us if we would like to go over to the boat show, we accepted readily. But not because we had any desire whatsoever to see the boats. No. We just thought it would be a nice change of pace to ride over to the East Coast for a day.

You see, on numerous occasions I had firmly announced that if I ever had to make a list of 100 things I'd most like to have, a boat of my own would be number 75.

And I always said that if and when I did ever buy a boat, I would insist on one with an indoor walk-in bathroom and a bed the kids could lie down on when they got tired or cranky. My husband used to take great comfort in this, knowing we would never have to worry because we'd never have that much money.

But in less than two hours after arriving at the boat show my desire for a beautiful new boat had catapulted right up there to No. 1. Not only did I have to have one, but I had to have one right away!

And I don't mind telling you, this is not like me. In the decade we've been married we have never bought a new model car. So you can imagine everyone's surprise when the urge to buy came over me.

Like the story of David and Goliath, it was not a big fancy sailboat or one of the gorgeous yachts that proved to be my downfall but a spiffy little 16-foot beauty with soft velour carpeting and powder blue and white interior -- my favorite color. Just what we need with two messy little kids, right?

No toilet. No bed. No nothing. But folks, the color is beautiful!

I almost bought the thing right on the spot -- one of those "boat show specials." But the voice of reason -- and my unbelievably shocked husband -- got hold of me and I decided to go home and think about it overnight.

However, at 4:30 the next morning I was sitting on the kitchen floor thumbing through the yellow pages trying to find someplace in my home town that sold my little boat.

By noon that day I was sitting in the marina. The kindly salesman must have known how to handle me because he didn't push me at all and I walked out with a great price on a bigger model instead and a number of special options. Oh, I couldn't wait.

I spent the next five days figuring out how I was going to come up with the money, and exactly one week after the boat show I was sitting at the marina again, this time ordering my boat.

My husband and kids are delighted with the situation especially since I managed to come up with the money on my own, but my husband said he is kicking himself for not taking me to a new car show instead!

The storm before the calm

People have always told me the two happiest days in the life of a boater are the day you buy the boat and the day you sell the boat. Recently I got to experience the first happy day. My "ship" finally came in.

The anticipation of waiting for your new boat to arrive is somewhat akin to awaiting for the birth of your first baby. You can't wait for it to happen but you are a little apprehensive about the "trip" down the canal.

My boat happened to be ready for "delivery" on a cold and windy Friday. The river was more than choppy -- it was rough. In fact, I half expected a tidal wave at any moment. But how could I wait another day to get the boat? No matter how bad the weather, I was determined to enjoy that first ride from the marina to my home.

About half way down the river I realized I should have bought a boat with a bathroom. When I get excited, so does my stomach. And my stomach didn't think that bouncing up and down on the river was the best way to spend a Friday afternoon. So I persuaded the captain -- that's what my husband likes to call himself now -- to make a potty stop at my parent's house and I took the car home while he drove the boat. I was humiliated, but my stomach was delighted.

The next day was different. The water was calm, the air was still, and I was ready to go. I was up early and packing a picnic lunch with visions of a full day of fun and sun.

After about five minutes in the water, I realized that things weren't always going to be smooth sailing. My youngest daughter was not thrilled about riding in the boat. In fact she started screaming the minute she got on, and she stopped screaming the minute she was carried off.

I'm not sure, but I think her screaming may have been the thing that led me to start screaming, and I'm sure my screaming was what started my husband screaming.

My daughter's screaming wasn't so noticeable when we were speeding down the river with the wind blowing in our ears. But as we pulled up to a dock to get gas, we had to slow the motor down. And that made the engine quieter and the screaming more apparent. Suddenly everyone on the dock was looking at us, trying to figure out what was the problem. And while everyone was looking at us, my husband was trying to figure out how to stop the boat before we crashed into the dock.

"Slow down," I yelled.

"I'm trying to," he shouted back. "This thing doesn't have any brake!"

"Turn the boat," I screamed. "We're going to hit the dock!"

"I am turning. But this doesn't work like my car," he shouted.

Then my other daughter joined in. "Stop yelling, you two."

"Don't get so tense," I yelled at my husband.

"I'm **NOT** tense!" he screamed, just after he shut the engine off.

By this time everyone on the dock was laughing, so I quickly put my daughter on the dock and she shut up. They're probably still talking about it.

We filled up the tank, my husband muttered something about the cost of living, and we shoved off from the dock. I tried to get my youngest daughter to wave at all the people watching us as we bounced off the pilings, but she wouldn't take time out from her screaming to open her eyes and look up.

"Isn't this a pleasant way to spend an afternoon?" I said as we headed quickly for home.

Once home we tossed the kids overboard to Grandma and headed out again. But this time things began to click.

We spent $4 worth of fuel practicing turning the boat around in the canal and after only an hour and a half we looked like we'd been doing it all our lives!

Then we headed for the river and, oh, was it great. My beautiful little boat just drove like a dream and when I sat

27

in the bow with the wind in my hair I couldn't imagine why I ever went so long without one. It's beautiful, it's exhilarating, and believe it or not, it's relaxing. I just can't wait until the kids calm down so we can all enjoy it!

High, but not dry

You don't know how exciting life in Florida can be until you've been shipwrecked, and then rescued by the U.S. Coast Guard.

I know it might sound like a funny story now, but at the time, believe me, I was scared stiff!

It all happened when my brother and his girlfriend made the mistake of offering to take my daughter, our visitor and me up to Cayo Costa for some good shelling.

My husband, who had work to do at home, offered to take care of the two little babies (little did he know what he was getting into!!) So we jumped at the chance, assuring him we would be back in about three or four hours.

Around 9 a.m., we climbed aboard my brother's boat, loaded down with fishing poles, towels, blankets and what seemed like enough food and drink for a week for an anxiously awaited picnic on the beach.

About an hour later Cayo Costa was within sight and my brother's 28-foot Chris Craft had just left the main channel and was cruising along at about 25 knots towards the island.

All at once we hit a sandbar. It was as though we had struck a brick wall. The boat came to an abrupt halt. We didn't. My friend, my daughter and I had been down in the cabin and the force of the impact threw us to the floor. I had grabbed onto the table to stop my fall, but the table ripped from the wall and landed on top of us!

The two in the back, who had somehow managed to break their fall, ran up to help us.

I was on top of the pile. I was sore but all right. My poor

little daughter who was caught in the middle was simply panicked. She was crying for help, but except for minor bruises was OK. My guest, who was on the bottom, was visibly shaken. The whiteness of her face made quite a contrast to the black and blue marks that were already beginning to form. We still didn't know what happened and we were all rather dazed.

All, that is, but my brother.

Never losing his cool for a moment, he jumped overboard to see what had happened. The rudder was bent but that wasn't all. The force of the impact had thrown the entire propeller and shaft right out through the back of the boat.

They were nowhere to be seen. Somehow, he got the boat off the sandbar.

Meanwhile, his girlfriend just then heard the sound of water coming from inside the boat. Not saying a word to us she quickly told my brother to get back on the boat because she thought we were taking on water.

She was right. The water was really starting to come in the bottom, but when my brother tried to turn on the engine to start the bilge pump, it would not start. We didn't know how large the hole was but there wasn't time to investigate. My brother yelled for the hand pump and as quickly as he could pump the water into a bucket, his girlfriend would toss it overboard.

My daughter kept crying, "Mommy, Mommy, we could have been killed," but I didn't hear her. I was scared to death we would have to jump out of the boat into those shark infested waters, but I said nothing.

"Don't panic," my brother kept repeating to his crew of four frantic women.

As the water began to empty out, he was able to see that the only hole was where the shaft was supposed to fit in, so he quickly plugged it up with his T-shirt. We were okay. We wouldn't sink.

We tried to reach the marine operator by radio for more than an hour, but she wouldn't answer. Finally he called the Coast Guard and asked them to phone my parents' home and ask whoever answered to come and tow us with their boat. About an hour later the Coast Guard called us back.

29

My parents' boat wouldn't work properly. They would send the Coast Guard Auxiliary boat, The Blue Runner, out to help us!

They didn't tell us it would be another hour and a half!

By this time everyone had started to relax and we were even beginning to laugh about the situation. We had our picnic on the boat. We were going to jump in and look for the prop, but we thought better of it. It was a wise decision.

We started to fish instead and believe it or not, the first thing we caught was a baby hammerhead shark! All we could think of was its mother and daddy and God-knows-who-else who must have been swimming around the boat hunting for their little "bundle of joy." We quickly threw it back.

Sometime after 2:30 p.m. The Blue Runner found us and started towing us slowly, carefully to Punta Rassa. On our 2½ hour journey back to the Sanibel bridge all we could think of was my husband stuck at home with two screaming babies, not knowing what had happened to the rest of his family.

We arrived back at our home at 6:30 p.m. to find two perfectly happy babies and a very relieved husband.

"Thank God you're back safely," he said.

He didn't know how right he was!

Middle age
and other spreads

To eat is human;
to digest, divine

After years of inner conflict I've finally decided -- God doesn't want me to be skinny!

No matter how good my intentions or how hard I try, whenever I decide to go on a diet something always comes up suddenly to bring it to an abrupt halt.

For example, I can go for week after week with absolutely nothing on my social calendar except the ink on the page. But let me decide to go on a diet and all of a sudden I'll be invited out for dinner four nights in a row!

And having company myself is as bad, if not worse. Everybody knows I like to cook so when I have visitors or out-of-town guests I like to come up with a little more than a plain piece of fish and some celery and carrot sticks. A little Hollandaise, a touch of Bernaise or maybe a small chocolate mousse for dessert couldn't hurt that much, right?

I am one of those people who was taught to eat everything on the plate. And I've been being a good girl doing what my mommy told me ever since.

When I was in my early 20s I went to the town physician well known for giving diet pills, and in no time I started losing weight like mad. The only problem was that I became a nervous wreck and my regular physician put me on mild tranquilizers for a while to try to calm me down. But even they didn't work.

Then I went to the druggist and asked him if he would put a few less tiny time pills in my diet capsules, but he refused. Well, I showed him! From then on I'd get my prescription, bring it home, pull each huge capsule apart and empty half of it down the drain.

One day my husband caught me and had a fit.

"What in the world are you doing? Those pills cost a fortune! Why bother getting them at all if you're going to throw them down the sink?" He was not thrilled.

So I decided enough was enough and tossed all my pills.

I guess it was about that time I decided to smoke a cigarette every time I wanted to put some food into my mouth. Smoking was fun. I enjoyed it. And it was a lot better than those awful diet pills.

But about a year later I found myself smoking three packs of cigarettes a day. I was coughing like crazy, my house reeked of smoke and my little girl had begun eating my stinky old cigarette butts like they were candy. Clearly I had to stop, and one day I did -- cold turkey.

But right away I noticed I was putting food in my mouth every time I wanted a cigarette.

I've been losing the battle of the bulge ever since.

Shortly before the birth of my first child, I lost my waist. And I've never been able to find it since.

A while back, I decided to give my ill-fated diet one last try. I determined that I couldn't let myself cheat or go off my diet for a single moment or I would get fed up with myself and forget the whole thing.

Well, would you believe it, two days later the powers-that-be decided that yours truly should start a restaurant review column! That did it. Cottage cheese tastes like cottage cheese no matter where you eat it and you don't want to read about that, right? Besides, I hate cottage cheese, and if I'm going to get to go out to a good restaurant I'll be darned if I'm going to stick to the "dieter's delight."

But the fatal blow came when an unbelievable French bakery opened nearby. Why, just walking into that store is like stepping foot on Fantasy Island. Even my husband has gone wild. He wouldn't get up early on Sunday morning if the Queen of England were coming to breakfast, but in the last few weeks he's practically broken his neck to get up and make it to the French bakery when it opens its doors Sunday at 8 a.m.! Why last Sunday we brunched on heavenly french bread, a delectable quiche, and a breakfast roll filled with chocolate that my husband "simply couldn't resist."

Once again my diet was a total disaster. Somehow, it's just not in the cards.

My eyes are always coming in contact with trouble

My eyes have always been a problem.

To be conservative, I would say that my eyes are on the same par as Mr. Magoo's. And when I was a teenager my parents decided that I was a definite candidate for contact lenses.

Contacts had just come out shortly before that and I don't mind telling you they were the rage. They were terribly expensive and terribly painful and when I wore them -- whenever I wore them -- I teared constantly. My eyes were so red I looked like a creature from outer space, but everyone was determined I would wear them.

One Friday several of my friends and I went to another girl's house for the evening and ended up spending the night. Since I hadn't planned on staying all night and didn't have my contact case with me, I couldn't figure out what to do with them when it was time for bed.

But soon I had a brainstorm that I felt was nothing short of genius. I waited until everyone else got in bed and then went into the bathroom.

I put the left lens in an empty soap dish, filled it with water and put it on the top shelf of the medicine cabinet. I put the right lens in the empty water glass, filled it with a little water and put it on top of the medicine cabinet too. Then I shut the cabinet door, told my friends what I had done and went to bed.

The next morning I awoke from sounds of utter confusion outside my bedroom door. When I got up and walked out I found everyone huddled around my best friend but when they saw me the nervous laughter ceased.

"Cathy has something she would like to tell you," my best friend's father said, trying to keep a straight face.

My friend looked pale as a ghost.

"Debby, I don't quite know how to tell you this, but I got sick in the middle of the night. I wanted to get rid of the taste in my mouth so I went to the medicine chest and got a drink of water. I'm afraid I drank your contact!"

Everyone in the whole house thought it was hysterical and pretty soon I was laughing too. Unfortunately my parents didn't see the humor, however, and I was in the dog house for months.

When I finally got my replacement contact I was scared stiff.

I knew if I lost them again I'd surely be grounded for the next 30 years. I was going to be careful.

One Sunday afternoon I decided to take a walk to the drive-in restaurant that was the teen hang-out. I wasn't going to take any chances this time so I took my empty case and my glasses with me just to be safe.

As I was walking along the sidewalk a cinder got in my eye so I decided to take out my contacts. I unscrewed the bottom of my lens-case and put in the left lens. Then I unscrewed the top and put in the other. I was about to put the case into my pocket but then decided to be extra safe and hook the chain with my identification tag on it through the belt loops on my slacks.

When I returned home several hours later wearing my glasses my parents were suspicious.

"Where are your contacts and why aren't you wearing them," my mother demanded.

"They're right here," I said indignantly, reaching for my contact case. My mother's face filled with horror.

There was the top of the case, just as I left it, hooked securely around my belt loop. But the rest of it had come unscrewed and both of my lenses were gone!

At that moment I gave up all hope of successfully wearing contacts. I figured if boys never made passes at girls who wear glasses, I'd just have to be content as a spinster.

But today, here I am, a happy mother of two, married to a man whose eyesight is even worse than my own. And we've made a few passes too, I dare say!

Now the only time we have trouble is when we try to go swimming.

For several years before the children came and I stopped working, my husband and I vacationed in the Virgin Islands, which has some of the most beautiful coral reefs, and therefore snorkeling, in the world.

Everyone down there would snork! Everyone, that is, except us. We couldn't see any of those colorful tropical fish unless they swam up and kissed us on the nose. It was depressing.

My husband finally got a regular snorkeling mask and lay in two inch deep water with his nose practically in the sand, waiting patiently until the little fish would pass by.

I, on the other hand, would lie on my towel, pretending not to know him, and I vowed that if I were ever lucky enough to return to the Virgin Islands again I would get a prescription snorkle mask.

Well folks, it was five years before we returned but this time we were prepared. We ordered prescription masks and oh, were they a sight. Prescription lenses were glued onto the inside of a regular swim mask and for the very first time we were able to discover the breathtaking beauty beneath the sea.

So if you're in the surf at Sanibel and happen to see two four-eyed monsters emerge from the sea, don't panic and scream and turn 'round and flee. It's probably just my husband, Mr. Magoo, and me.

With a wig and a prayer

You don't know what a curse naturally curly hair can be until you've spent your whole life trying to get rid of a fine frizzy dishwater blonde afro!

I mean while all the other girls went through life with the hair style of the year like the page boy, pixie, shag, long straight look and finally the Farrah Fawcett "do," yours truly always managed to walk out of the house looking like she just shook hands with Reddy Kilowatt. I'm telling you, it was the pits!

At first it wasn't so bad. I was little and my "cute little ringlets" were the envy of every little old lady I met. My hair was so soft and curly that complete strangers couldn't resist the urge to come up and pat me on the head just so they could get to feel it.

Then they would invariably tell me how lucky I was and how they spent dollar after dollar trying to get their hair to look like mine. And, after hearing it time and again, I began to believe it.

But then puberty set in and I was dealt a crushing blow. The nice soft locks that used to adorn my head were getting tighter and tighter and tighter. One day I looked in the mirror and discovered to my horror that my head was now covered with hundreds of tightly coiled springs! In addition to that, the beautiful light blonde color was getting darker by the day and I thought I'd never go out of the house again.

Something had to be done.

When I was 14 I decided to take the bull by the horns and try to set it on rollers. I'd spend hours putting it up in those miserable thorny brush rollers and when I'd take it down I'd be gorgeous. But the very second I'd walk outside in the humidity, or rain, or snow, or heat, the spell would be broken and there I'd be with instant frizzies! Oh, was it humiliating.

My friends, on the other hand, found it simply fascinating. Time after time one would take up the challenge and try to "do something with Debby's hair." I remember one occasion when one of them wet my hair and then pulled a stocking over it to keep it straight. When the hair dried and the stocking came off everyone burst into hysterics. I looked just like that bust of Julius Caesar in our Latin classroom!

My sister also got into the act and took me down to the basement, where she did her best to iron it. We had heard it worked great for girls with long hair, but since mine was only two or three inches long it was a disaster. Not only did it not work, but she kept hitting my head with the iron and it burned like mad.

At times like those I would consider shaving it all off, but immediately I'd think of what my grandfather told me. It seems he, too, had thin problem hair and he had heard sometime in his late teens that if he'd shave it all off it would grow in thicker. Well, he gave it a try. Instead, it never grew back and he was bald as a billiard ball until the day he died!

Sometime around the age of 15 I decided to go to the professionals and tell them my problem. They suggested that I have my hair straightened. It sounded like the answer to my prayers -- a few hours at the beauty parlor and I was to have straight hair for four to six months. I couldn't say yes fast enough. For the next two days I thought I was lovely. But on the third day it started to rain outside and the frizzies were at it again! I was heartsick. The beauticians were shocked. And my friends found it too funny for words. After waiting until it was safe, the hairdresser tried to straighten it again. This time it lasted a little over three weeks. I was crushed.

Well, it was back to the rollers for the next few years until one Christmas my sister made the fatal mistake of giving me a wig. Many people had suggested it before but I had taken it as the supreme insult and would never even consider it.

I was really hurt when I opened that present but, trying not to let it show, I reluctantly agreed to go with her into the room and let her try to fix it. When she was done and made me look into the mirror I simply couldn't believe it. I felt like a miracle had occurred. Not only was I straight and stylish at last, but I was blonde and beautiful as well!

I'm really ashamed to admit it, but I wore a wig on my head every day for the next three years. Nobody ever saw me without my wig except my husband. And everybody seemed to like it except my parents and grandparents who will forever hold a sentimental attachment to "those beautiful ringlets" of days gone by.

However, when they stopped making the style of wig I'd been wearing it was time to reassess my situation. I had to admit I was overdoing it a bit. So it was back to the rollers for day-to-day use and my new wig was adorned whenever the frizzies reared their ugly heads. And, thanks to L'Oreal, the dishwater blonde was never seen again!

Well, all went well for many years until we moved to Florida. Need I say more? If I would have stayed in the house every day I had the frizzies down here I would have become more of a recluse than Howard Hughes! And to make matters even worse, wearing a wig in this heat is simply unbearable.

Needless to say, something had to be done. So once again I turned to the professionals.

First of all no one could believe that anyone with a natural afro would want to get rid of it. It was so stylish. So chic. So when I looked around the shop I could understand their dismay. Almost everyone in there who didn't already have the frizzies in one form or another was there trying to get them.

But after telling them the story of my life they were more than understanding. Yes, new ways had been developed to straighten the hair and they would be glad to try it on me.

Well, fellow Floridians, I'll have you know that my hair is blonde and beautiful once again! I've had it done many times since I've been here and each time I marvel at the thrill of having my hair do what I want it to do for a change. Each time I walk outside on a humid day, or go to the beach, or get caught in the rain, I still find myself running to the mirror to make sure it hasn't frizzed up. And when I find that all is well, I feel like I've pulled one over on the world. It's one battle I'll never have to fight again.

Did you ever know a dentist who didn't hum?

Some people tremble at ghost stories.

Others are horrified by murder mysteries.

But when I'm in the room those things pale in comparison if someone inadvertently brings up that terror of terrors -- the dentist!

Chills run up and down my spine. Perspiration drips from every pore and thousands of little men with sledge hammers start pounding in my head! Immediately, I can smell that unmistakable odor, and the whirr of that high speed drill starts humming in my ears. It's all I can do not to throw up!

And then, right before my eyes, is a vision of old Herbert the Hacker, himself, humming away, poised and preparing to pounce with his pick.

Herbert, you see, was a demon in dental disguise. And, unfortunately, he was my dentist.

When I was growing up, going to the dentist could be a mighty frightening thing at best. And good old Herbert saw to it that I got to savor every terrifying moment of it.

His office was on the ninth floor of a big old office building and as soon as the elevator door opened on that floor, that awful, unmistakable odor was there to greet me. As I'd follow my nose down the hall, I would then be met by the sound of screaming children and a low-pitched hum and I knew in a moment it must be old Herb. (I've since decided that humming must be the first thing they teach in Dentistry 101).

As I'd sit down during the usual half hour wait, too nervous to concentrate on the ragged and torn magazines that I had read some six months ago, I sometimes would secretly glance around to see if the other adults and teenagers were as panicked as I was.

Then when the tension had reached its peak, a girl would walk in and announce, "Debby, Dr. Herb will see you now!"

Then the terror would really begin. The dental hygienists who cleaned my teeth were always recent graduates from a nearby college with very little experience and who didn't seem to think they were really getting my teeth clean unless they drew at least a half pint of blood from my gums at the same time. Oh were they rough!

But compared to Dr. Herb they were a godsend.

Then the moment of truth would finally arrive when Dr. Herb would walk in with his usual half smile and sing-song voice and his eyes gleaming at the thought of another victim sitting in his chair.

Of course, yours truly always had a million and one cavities so I would have appointments stretched out over the next four months.

Dr. Herb's tools were attracted to a nerve like a piece of metal to a magnet and when the nurse placed the drill in that man's hands, she might as well have given him a jackhammer.

I would beg and plead with him to numb me to death, but no matter how many shots he'd give me, he would still darn near kill me with pain.

When I was 18 and off to college, I swore I'd never go again.

It wasn't until 10 years later that I started to worry about my teeth. I dreamed one night that all my teeth rotted and fell out and I woke up screaming in terror.

We had since moved to a new town and I decided I had better reassess my position. I started asking around.

Practically everyone I knew, old and young alike, were singing the praises of Dr. Harry Glatz. It seemed Dr. Glatz was a kind and gentle man who taught transactional analysis throughout the community in his spare time and practiced it in his office. He was determined to make his patients feel calm and relaxed in his care. (Besides that he had a marvelous analgesia machine that I had never used but it was supposed to do wonders to calm the nerves!)

But I was still a little leery and was not about to take anybody's word. I decided to check him out. First of all I appeared anonymously at some of his lectures. Not bad. Then I sent my husband and daughter in for a little dental work and they both came back with glowing reports. Then I called his nurse and talked to her and she thought he might be just the one for me.

Upon her suggestion I made an appointment to come in and talk to him. They could clean my teeth and we could talk and after that it was up to me. Well, that sounded pretty fair, so off I went.

In his cheery waiting room, instead of tattered books there were photo albums of all his little patients, sitting in the dentist's chair -- SMILING LIKE MAD! Good psychology! Then his receptionist brought me a cup of coffee and before I was finished I was ready.

When I got in the chair I was scared to death. But when they put a napkin in my lap for my sweaty hands as well as the one around my neck I got my first inkling that they might truly understand.

My teeth were cleaned before I knew it with absolutely no pain. Then he walked in and we talked. He showed me the nitrous oxide machine and tried it on me so I could see how it felt.

"Okay doc," says I, "I'll make you a deal. If you numb me like mad and really gas me up, I'll let you work on my teeth. But the first time you hurt me our deal is off."

"Fine," said he, without hesitation, and our wonderful relationship began.

My cavities were quite extensive after almost a dozen years, and yet that man never hurt me once! Each time after filling a particularly large cavity, he or his nurse would phone me the next day to make sure I was okay and not having any pain.

I got to the point where I almost liked going to the dentist. This was one relationship I was determined never to end.

Then we moved to Florida. Dear God, what was I going to do?

Well, folks, I'm ashamed to say I haven't been to a dentist since. But how could I ever find a dentist again who soothes my nerves, has a gas machine, calls me on the phone and causes me no pain?

I've finally come up with a solution. This is just the excuse I've been waiting for to go back north every year.

4

You've got to be kidding!

If I could just change my name!

I've decided that being a mother is like being a doctor -- you're always on call.

For years I longed to hear a little voice calling out "mommy!" Now all I yearn for is a few minutes of silence.

All day long the kids are crying **"MOMMY!!"** It's usually followed by **"come here, quick!!"**

It starts early in the morning, just before the sun comes up. Even though my 3-year-old's room is on the other side of the house, I can hear her call as if she were standing next to my bed.

"Mommy! Potty!"

Those magic words push me out of bed. If I don't get her to the bathroom, she'll never learn to go without a diaper at night, I say to myself as I grope through the kitchen and try to find her room in the darkness.

"Mommy! Water!"

Why doesn't anyone else in the house hear her call, I keep asking myself at 5:30 in the morning. How can my husband sleep through her screams, I wonder.

"Mommy! Up!"

I know she'll never go back to sleep, so I finally go in and get her out of the crib. If I were smart, I would leave the sides down so she could get out herself. But then, she would have free run of the house, and there's no telling what I would find each morning -- syrup on the floor; cereal on the rug; toys in the dishwasher; toothpaste on the toilet. It's better to keep her confined.

"Mommy! Bib!"

44

When she hands me her bib and demands that it be tied around her neck, it's time for breakfast. She mixes a little egg with the milk, and then a little milk with the toast, and then a little toast with cereal, and then a little of the whole mixture with the rug.

"Mommy! Off!"

That means she's through with breakfast and it's time to take the tray off the high chair and let her down. If I'm not quick enough, she starts to stand up, and that means the whole glass of milk will tip over on the rug. Do you remember what milk on rug smells like two days later?

"Mommy! Play!"

She stands in front of the television, effectively blocking the view. If she doesn't want me to watch TV, there's no use fighting it. She wins every time.

"Mommy! Read!"

She pulls the newspaper out of my hands and plops down on my lap with one of her little books. Usually it is the same book -- the one about the baby duck. I have that story etched in my memory. I don't even have to look at the pages anymore, unless she wants to read it backwards.

"Mommy! Outside!"

It's time to get the mail from the mail box. Somehow she can hear the mailman drive by. His truck must sound different. She never misses it.

"Mommy! Over!"

The flower vase has mysteriously tipped over and the water is streaming down the leg of the table. She grabs about 30 paper towels and tries to help.

"Mommy! Help!"

She's stuck behind the chair and she is panicked.

"Mommy! In!"

I've closed the bathroom door for a minute's peace, and she doesn't like it a bit.

"Mommy! Bug!"

She found a raisin that dropped off her sister's toast and she's horrified.

"Mommy! Elament!"

She's just seen an elephant on the television, and I've got to see it with her.

45

"Mommy! Shoes!"

She has put on a pair of my shoes and is pleased that she looks grown up, even though she's stumbling all over the house.

"Mommy!"

So it goes all day long. If I could change my name for a few hours, I would welcome the chance.

"Mommy! Kiss!"

But how can a mother get tired of seeing her baby's smile or feeling the little tug on the hand and the hug around the leg.

"Mommy! Love you!"

Harmony and discord

Watch out, America. Background music is coming to the foreground, and taking over.

I never really noticed how much canned music has influenced my life until last week when we took our kids out to dinner.

You haven't truly known hostility until you walk into a nice restaurant with an 8-year-old and a 3-year-old. As the hostess shows you to a table in a remote corner of the dining room, normally gracious diners raise their eyebrows in anger at the sight of two children.

I know in my own mind that each one breathes a sigh of relief as we move along to a table farther away. And I guess I can't blame them. After all, some of my own relatives have the same reaction. Why should some small children ruin a perfectly delightful dinner?

I didn't let that bother me. My kids were pretty good that night. But everything they said seemed to take on a louder tone than normal. It was almost as if a hush fell over the room. My daughter's remarks seemed to carry to every corner of the restaurant.

It was then that I realized there was no background music in the restaurant. The melodic notes that normally

come through those little vents in the ceiling weren't
working that night. And oh, how quiet it was!

"Mommy, I want roast beef," my 8-year-old said.

I could feel dozens of eyes focusing on me when I quietly
insisted she have something a little less expensive.

"But mommy, I'm sick of chicken. I want roast beef!"
she told everyone who would listen.

"We'll discuss it later," I said with a forced smile.

My 3-year-old doesn't know how to say roast beef, thank
goodness. But she does know how to say "mine!" with such
force that most of the things she points to usually do
become hers.

"Mine!" she said, pointing to the water. "Mine!" she
said, pointing to the rolls. "Mine!" she said, pointing to her
sister's salad.

The first few "mines" are always cute. But it gets a little
monotonous. I wanted to stand up and announce "this child
is **not mine!**" But I knew if I did, my daughter would point
at me and shout "mine!"

Somehow, with that distracting background music, such
scenes don't seem quite so bad. At least not quite so loud.
But without Mantovani's orchestra in the background, the
conversation at our table became part of the conversation
at the next table. It wasn't a comfortable situation!

I guess we have come to depend on Muzak in our daily
routines.

When you board a jet plane, you don't hear the sound of
roaring engines. You are greeted by the sounds of a
Hawaiian luau.

When you make a bank deposit, you count out your
money to the beat of Andre Kostelanetz.

The other day I was calling the doctor's office and they
put me on hold. All of a sudden I heard Xavier Cugat's
orchestra serenading me over the phone.

It doesn't really bother me to have all this music forced
on me every day of the week. But I'm beginning to notice
that some people are having a hard time with Muzak with-
drawal symptoms.

The other day I was at the beach and I saw a jogger

47

running along the shore. Strapped to his chest was a radio, and covering his ears were headphones. I guess he was running to the beat of a different drummer.

"You never told me about Ultra-Brite!"

When I was a little girl about my daughter's age, I firmly believed I was Irish because my great-aunt's birthday was on St. Patrick's Day.

I guess I wasn't the brightest kid when I was growing up. Until I was 7 and found out otherwise, I always thought my father, who each year worked on the Community Chest's Red Feather Drive, sold red feathers for a living! Now that I think of it, it's no wonder I had so much trouble with logic when I got to college.

But I wasn't the only child to have a little problem with logic. Almost every child I meet, be it on the job or at home, can mix a little imagination with some not-so-sound reasoning and come up with some real beauties.

For example, several months ago I was talking to some of the children in our neighborhood about Thanksgiving and the Pilgrims. One blonde, 7-year-old cutie seemed especially knowledgeable on the subject so I asked her why the Pilgrims ever decided to give up their homes in Europe and leave all their friends to come over and live in a strange country like America.

"Well," she said, almost in a huff, "they certainly didn't want their kids to grow up and speak Dutch!" Heaven forbid!

Another of my favorites involves a thoughtful father who took his daughter to work with him for several hours one day so that she could see first hand what his job entailed.

When she came home that day she was so impressed with her daddy. Not because he was editor of a newspaper. No way.

"Mommy," she boasted, "he's the only one in his whole office with his very own paste pot!"

Another little boy I grew up with always thought his daddy was a barber because he cut his son's hair each month.

One thing I'll always treasure is a note I received recently. You see, our kids got a gym set for Christmas but I told the other neighborhood children that they couldn't climb up on top of the monkey bars unless they had their parent's permission.

One imaginative 9-year-old came back late that afternoon with a crumpled piece of note paper.

There, in writing that could only belong to a child, I read:

"Yes, as long as she is careful and doesen't break her neck. Ha. Ha.

Signed
Mrs. ------"

Oh, how I love it.

But one of my most unforgettable moments came when my older daughter was about 3 years old and the two of us were taking a walk around the block one crisp fall day.

I remember we were walking along slowly hand-in-hand and I was feeling especially maternal that day. Suddenly she became fascinated with the falling leaves and she asked me to explain it to her.

I was thrilled and tried so hard to explain this marvelous wonder of nature in simple terms that she would understand and always remember. I thought I had done a particularly good job and as we walked the rest of the way in silence I wondered what was going through her little mind as she looked so pensively studying the trees.

Suddenly she stopped, tugged at my hand and looked right up to my eyes.

"Mother," she said in such a tone that I knew this was going to be one of those precious moments of motherhood that I would always cherish, "You never told me about Ultra Brite!"

The gumball
theory of economics

I've been reading a lot lately about how we should teach our children to manage money -- even at the age of 5.

That's an interesting thought, and I couldn't agree more. But obviously the experts giving us this sage bit of advice are unmarried economists who lost contact with childhood three decades ago.

Anyone who deals with 5-year-olds on a daily basis knows that anything you can teach them about money management goes out the window as soon as a child walks past a gumball machine.

Let's be honest, folks. How many of you have ever seen a child leave a supermarket without throwing a temper tantrum after spying the gumball machine?

I can describe the scene better than I can describe my own kitchen. The mother and child are in the checkout line with a cart full of cereal, cookies, soda, candy bars and ice cream. They have just done battle over whether the child can get a pack of bubble gum from the display rack that is always in front of the cash register. The mother has handed over a $50 bill for one bag of groceries, and is staggering from shock. The two head toward the door when suddenly the little boy sees a row of gumball machines.

"Mommy, can I have a penny?"

The woman says "No dear, all these machines take nickels and quarters."

"Mommy, can I have a quarter?"

The woman calmly answers, "No, son, that's too much to spend on a piece of junk that I'll end up throwing away this afternoon."

"Mommy, why can't I have a quarter? Tommy's mother always lets him have a quarter."

The mother, slightly frustrated, says "Tommy's mother can afford it, but I can't. Let's go home."

"Mommy, you never let me have anything!"

The mother, trying to keep the rage inside her, says,

"But dear, what about all this cereal? What about this nauseating candy? What about the Star Wars lunch box? What about that football? What about that $75 bike?" By this time she realizes she is screaming at the child and 15 customers have turned around to watch.

"Mommy, can I have a nickel?" the child asks.

By now the mother is flushed with anger and humiliated because everyone in the store knows what a terrible mother she is. So she hands him a nickel and angrily says, "Here, now hurry up!" Come to think of it, maybe children do know a lot about money management!

When I was a child, gumball machines only took pennies. And cherry slushes were only a nickel. And I think it was easier for kids then because there just weren't that many things for children to buy.

But today my daughter's $1 allowance won't go very far. And try explaining inflation to an 8-year-old. I try to encourage her to save her allowance so that she will have enough money to buy something nice, but she prefers to spend it as she gets it on things like bubble gum cards and ice cream cones. And of course, gumball machines.

That's why I was interested in seeing what the "experts" advised in teaching kids to respect money. They think parents should help children to make rational decisions, and help them realize that there will always be a scarcity problem and that our wants always exceed our needs. They also suggest that parents take children to stores to let them watch you make the buying decisions.

Good advice, I'm sure. But whenever I take my kids shopping, we always end up fighting. Their choices always tend to be the wrong choices.

If we are shopping for clothes and the choice is between a $9 blouse (white with a cute little collar) or a $9 T-shirt (pink with a large picture of Miss Piggy printed across the front) my daughter will invariably choose the T-shirt. And then we go through the "gumball machine" routine.

The way I see it, the only thing my children learn from going shopping with me is that money always leads to arguments. I guess they are learning one important economic principle, however -- money is the root of all evil!

5

The family that stays together deserves a medal

Something to chew on

Dinner at our house is always a disaster.

It's so bad that a TV camera crew stopped by last week to film our dinner for "That's Incredible."

For some reason, I always thought that when I had children, we would gather around the table every night, and break bread in a civilized manner. Something like a Norman Rockwell painting, if you know what I mean.

Well, Norman painted the wrong picture when he got around to meal time at my house.

The trouble starts before the food even gets to the table.

"Turn the TV off and go wash your hands," I tell my oldest daughter as I pull the meat out of the oven and mash the potatoes.

"What'd you say, Mom?" she asks every night, as if there could possibly be some new direction that she hasn't heard seven days a week, 52 weeks a year for the past eight years.

By the time the TV is turned off and her hands are actually clean, her dinner is a bit cold.

"Go get your bib and sit in your high chair," I tell my 3-year-old as I pour the milk and cut the meat.

But she doesn't want to sit in her high chair. She thinks she is old enough to sit in a regular chair like the rest of us. The fact that she can't even see over the top of the table doesn't seem to have an influence on her judgment at all.

By the time all the preliminary arguments about clean hands and seating arrangements have been taken care of and the four of us sit down to eat, we are all ready for some serious arguments.

54

It usually starts out with: "Well, what did you do at school (or camp, or work, or the store) today?" That question, known at our house as "THE QUESTION," can be asked of anyone by anyone.

But no matter who asks THE QUESTION, the answer is always: nothing.

THE QUESTION is usually followed by THE OTHER QUESTION: Well, what's new at school (or camp, or work, home) this week.

THE OTHER QUESTION always gets the same ANSWER: nothing.

When THE QUESTIONS are out of the way we get down to the basics.

"I don't like this meat."

"Do I have to eat those yucckky vegetables?"

"Why can't we watch TV during dinner?"

"She has more fruit salad than I have!"

"Don't you dare spill that milk again!"

"Why can't we have what I like to eat?"

"I'm full. No room for vegetables."

"If you want dessert, you'd better eat everything."

Now these statements aren't made in the normal tone of voice. They are either in the form of a whine, a plea, a loud demand, a cry of frustration, or an angry shout. The one thing they all have in common is that they are loud.

My husband, who for some strange reason always turns on soothing music as we sit down at the table each night, usually ends up turning the radio off, either because he can't hear the music or because he thinks the music drives the children to shout louder than they normally do. So much for Mantovani.

"Don't eat the rice with your fingers!"

"What is this green stuff in the noodles?"

"Sit up straight and get your feet off the table!"

"There's the doorbell. I'll get it!"

"You can't leave this house until you clean off your plate!"

About halfway through dinner each night my youngest daughter announces that she has to go to the potty. It never fails. No matter that she just went to the bathroom minutes before dinner. We clean her off, take her out of her chair, and wait.

My theory is that there is a little clock in her --- well never mind my theory.

"Oops, the milk spilled again."

"All four legs of that chair belong on the floor!"

"Ellen's having something good for dinner tonight. I wish I were at her house."

"I wish you were too!"

"Don't eat that napkin."

After all the questions and quarrels during dinner time, dessert is a real treat. By dessert time I don't even hear the complaints. I have just one thing on my mind -- dirty dishes.

Sitting there at the dining room table, staring at the half-empty plates and the puddle of milk, the sliced carrots hidden under the placemat and the rice buried in the shag carpet, it's hard to remember that there were actually peaceful meals. Meals with wine and fresh flowers, with linen napkins and real silver. Meals with stimulating conversation. In other words, meals without children.

How to survive a vacation

Packing the kids in the car and taking a two-week family vacation is one of my favorite things in life.

On my list of all-time great highs, it comes right after cleaning the toilet bowls and right before ironing a dozen white shirts.

Somehow the family "vacation" always leaves me frustrated, exhausted and broke.

The frustration usually begins one or two days before we are to leave. That's when one of the kids gets sick. It can range from simple diarrhea to complex ear infections.

If it's just diarrhea, the child will probably be well by the time we reach Atlanta. If it's an ear infection, well you just might as well plan spending the entire two weeks shouting.

Also before we leave there is the simple matter of packing the suitcases. Out of a family of four, I seem to be the only one who knows how to pack a suitcase.

My husband thinks that getting the empty suitcases out of the attic and arranging the packed suitcases in the trunk of the car is his only responsibility. So he's out of the picture.

My oldest daughter has trouble picking out which clothes to take with her. If we were going to Alaska, she would take three swimsuits, sandals, and a pair of shorts. If we were going to Miami, she would take sweaters, heavy pants, and perhaps some mittens. The rest of the suitcase would be filled with toys.

After we get the clothes packed and the car loaded with books, toys, stuffed animals, soft drinks, snacks, lunch for the first day, maps, tissues, and a tour guide book, it's time to squeeze into the old sedan and hope that it will make it.

If we are driving any distance at all, the first day isn't too bad. The kids have plenty to read and they're still excited about a new experience.

The second day is maddening, however. I always thought the solution would be to install one of those glass windows that partitions the front seat from the back seat. I would sell my soul for one of those windows. The front seat would be quiet and comfortable. You could see what was happening in the back seat, if you cared to look, but you wouldn't be disturbed.

Then there's the seating arrangement. If one kid is in the front seat, the other one wants to be there, too. If they are both in the front seat and I'm in the back seat, they want to be there, too. If I'd known that vacations were going to be like this, I'd have bought a car with four seats in the front and no back seat at all.

That's part of the exhaustion. After two weeks I'm so tired of settling disputes and answering questions, I could scream. But I doubt anyone would hear me.

Life in a series of motels is no treat, either. Four people just weren't meant to sleep in the same room together, especially when two of them are children. I guess that's how one-night-stands came about.

I don't know about you, but I get absolutely no sleep on a vacation. It's as if someone said "make sure she doesn't get any rest and relaxation."

Once we get where we're going, there's the big battle about where we're going to stay. My husband likes apartments or condos because they have kitchens and "we save a lot of money by not eating out."

Some big treat. If I wanted to cook meals and wash dishes on my vacataion, I would have suggested a camper.

"So when does my vacation begin?" I usually ask him.

His answer is always the same: "If you want to pay for going out to dinner, be my guest."

The trip home is about the same scenario, but at a greater level of frustration.

So this year, when the topic of vacations came up, I suggested something different.

"Instead of taking a family trip this summer, let's stay close to home. We've got the beach and the sunshine in our own back yard, so let's take advantage of it."

We took a vote and Sanibel won. Actually, we all won. No fights, no long drive, no frazzled nerves.

A week at Sanibel is the perfect way to survive your vacation. If it doesn't rain!

Never travel without
a pediatrician in your suitcase

There's no place like home for the holidays, it's true.

But when you're traveling up North with two sick kids stuffed into an old car overflowing with luggage and gifts, you begin to wonder if it's really worth it.

For well over a year, I had been dreaming of a white Christmas surrounded by old friends and mountains of snow. And truly, that part of the trip was even better than I had imagined.

But now that it's over I sometimes think I should have had my head examined!

The following account of our disastrous Christmas vacation is all true. In fact, I'm leaving some of the more gruesome details out -- they're just too horrible to mention!

I got my first inkling that things might not go exactly as planned even before we left when our youngest daughter developed an ear infection. Off to the pediatrician we went and were assured that if we took the medicine for 10 days we should have no problem. (If he but knew!)

I don't know quite how to put this delicately but the day we left she developed a terrible case of, well, the trots. Need I say more?

You talk about gross! I spent the first day of my dream vacation in the crammed back seat of the car changing not only diapers but entire outfits as well.

The second day we had decided to go out of our way and visit some friends who live in Asheville, N.C. We planned to arrive around dinner time and spend the night and the next day with them. Sounds nice, eh?

But when we arrived at their house there was a note on the door. They had tried to phone us but we had just left. Her father had a massive coronary and they were on their way to Florida!

That night in the motel the baby got worse. So early next morning I phoned the local emergency room and they said to bring her in. The doctor there said her ear was fine and took her off her medicine. Mistake No.1.

From there on in we had a doctor in every port!

By the time we arrived at my sister's in West Virginia the next night, the baby seemed better but my other daughter had a temperature of 105!

After being up all night trying in vain to get her temperature down, I asked my sister if we could go with her when she took her little boy to the doctor's that morning for a bad cold. The doctor prescribed some big pink, chewable tablets for both the kids and spent a good 20 minutes stressing the importance of them taking their medicine.

When we got home yours truly decided to calm the boy's fears by having him watch my 7-year-old take her pill first.

"Here," I said. "Just watch Beth. They're good."

With that my daughter took one bite, choked, and the half

59

eaten tablet went flying into the sink. By now the boy was backed up flat against the wall, saying, "I'm not going to take that pill. No way!"

"Nonsense," I replied. "Beth just had a cough. Here, I'm going to give her another one. Just watch how she loves it."

I popped the pill into my poor daughter's mouth and when she started gagging I knew I was in trouble. But when she saw my nasty, stern look she continued chewing until all of a sudden up it came, lunch and all, all over the kitchen!

Talk about pandemonium! My daughter was standing there crying her eyes out. The little boy ran away shaking in terror, screaming, "I'll never take that pill. I'll never take that pill," and my baby was giggling with delight over the whole affair. What a zoo.

From then on things improved somewhat (how could they get worse?) until Christmas Day when the baby started crying again and pulling at her ears.

The next day we drove to our old home town in New York, and I phoned my old pediatrician and told him my tale of woe. He prescribed another antibiotic for the baby and I thought we were home free. What a dreamer!

New York had been showered with over 20 inches of snow on Christmas Day so it looked like a fairy land. I was in heaven there, going to the dentist, playing in the snow and visiting dear friends.

But three days later, when we arrived in Buffalo to spend New Year's with friends, our troubles began again. Our two youngest children -- only a month apart -- fought like cats and dogs over everything. They cried constantly.

To make matters worse we had to sleep in the same room as the baby, so when she was up all night crying from her earache, so were we.

On Jan. 2, my husband and my older daughter, who had to be back for school, started to drive home but had to stop a day in Pittsburgh to get the car fixed. It wouldn't start!

I, on the other hand, had been given a surprise Christmas present of an extra week up North with the baby and an airline ticket home!

So, off to my old home town we went in a little rented car.

We arrived around 7 p.m. on a Saturday night at the home of friends who had offered their home while they were vacationing in the Caribbean. It was late but I decided to call my old pediatrician again to give him an update on the baby's condition.

Within a half hour, I was back at the emergency room again! It seems the medication had not affected her in the least and the infection was completely out of control. He gave her a shot, changed her medication and finally we were on the road to recovery.

It was then and there I made my vow.

I will never -- ever -- go on a trip again without a pediatrician in my suitcase!

Can America survive
without the blow-dry look?

There has been a lot of bad news in the world recently. But the most depressing news story got buried on the inside pages. The top hair dresser in the nation has predicted that the blow-dry hair style is on its way out.

I don't mind telling you, the shock waves are still rumbling.

The hair stylist, a woman from Alabama who broke all records at the National Beauty Show competition and is now first on the USA Hairdressing Team, said the blow-dryer is fading from the American scene.

She claims that women want to return to the hair set, and that will be the trend of the 1980s.

If that's true, my hair dryer is in for a surprise. With four people in our house -- three of them female -- the blow dryer is in use morning, noon and night. It spit out its last asbestos three years ago and has been going strong ever since.

Come to think of it, my daughters have actually grown up with the blow-dry look. As soon as they get out of the tub, they know the first thing you reach for is the hair dryer.

Click ... click ... click ... click! And we're off and drying.

With each click, the dryer gets hotter, and as it gets hotter, it gets louder. In no time at all the piercing, screaming high-pitched whine from the bathroom reaches through the entire house.

No sooner does one person put it down than another picks it up.

Click ... click ... click ... click! "It's my turn, mother!"

Somewhere through the steamy mist covering the bathroom mirror, you can see my oldest daughter carefully combing her blond curls with hot air.

I've always justified it in my own mind as being healthy to send my daughters to bed with warm dry hair, rather than let them sit around with damp hair for an hour before going to bed. Of course, that excuse seemed a lot more rational when we were living up north in the winter, where it was possible to catch a cold.

Click ... click ... click ... click! With each click the little wheel on our electric meter picks up speed. Soon it is whirling around so fast that it is just a blur.

I suppose if the blow-dry look is really on its way out, we can save some money on electric bills. Come to think of it, maybe that hair dresser's forecast was simply a ploy to get the nation to save on energy. I bet she was a government agent, tricking the people of this great blown-dry nation.

If we soon start to see advertising campaigns and editorials claiming that each "hot comb" uses up the equivilent of three barrels of oil a year, I will be pretty suspicious.

The sun may be good for drying clothes, but nothing works better on hair than a good old American (or Japanese) hair dryer. You can pull the plug on my iron or my vacuum cleaner. But you're not going to take away the blow-dry look without a fight. After all, everyone knows that the wet head is dead!

⑥

Growing pains
at 35

I wasn't really prepared to send my kid to camp!

Sending a kid off to camp is like learning how to swim.

No matter how well prepared you think you are, you don't know what it is really all about until you actually take the plunge!

For years, I've been living for the time that my oldest daughter would reach the ripe old age of 8 and be able to go off and experience the fun and frolics of a day camp. (In all candor I must admit that the thought of spending a couple weeks in the summer without having to listen to that mournful chant, "Mom, there's nothing for me to do," also crossed my mind.)

So it was with great anticipation that I sent my daughter off, lunchbox in hand, to her first day at camp. As I watched her bus pull away I could hardly bear the excitement - - she was free, I was free. What a vacation this would be!

But, instead of spending my first free day at the beach or shopping, I found myself sitting at home from 7:30 a.m. until 4 p.m. waiting for that dreaded phone call I was sure would come, informing me that my daughter had broken her leg, or had been bitten by a snake, had broken out from head to toe with poison ivy, or had been in a bus accident.

You see, long ago my sister had broken her leg at camp and I had prepared myself for the worst.

Everytime the phone rang, my heart skipped a beat. The clock seemed to be moving in slow motion. Maybe she was scared. She didn't know anyone. Maybe she was standing in a corner all alone with nobody else to play with.

I drove to her camp bus stop 10 minutes early, only to have the bus come 25 minutes late. My only consolation was that some of the other mothers looked just as nervous as I was.

Finally, she jumped off the bus, filthy dirty but grinning from ear to ear.

"Mother," she said, "It was so neat. They have smelly sulphur water and terrible outdoor toilets and we made crafts and I love it!"

As soon as she got home, she ran to the bathroom -- she hadn't gone all day because she was afraid to use the outhouse toilets!

Later that night, she volunteered to sing one of the new songs she learned at camp. It began:

"She waded in the water and she got her toes all wet, she waded in the water and she got her toes all wet, she waded in the water and she got her toes all wet, but she didn't get her woo-woo wet!" At that point, she jumped around, stuck her little bottom out and shook it like mad.

I thought my husband was going to croak. Good heavens, had she grown up in just one day?

But we breathed a collective sigh of relief as she continued her song, each verse changing the word "toe" for another spot higher up the leg. When she mistakenly said "cows" for calves and "sighs" for thighs, we knew she was still our little girl. Then she giggled like mad in the last verse when the "woo-woo" was finally changed to bathing suit!

From that moment on, I began to relax. But she came home several days later and announced that the following day they would be allowed to camp out overnight if their parents gave them permission.

She was absolutely beside herself with excitement and had a list of at least 20 items that she just had to take.

This was new to me and I was more than a little apprehensive, but after checking with a number of other mothers and the camp, I decided to let my 8-year-old go.

The big day arrived and she had so many things to carry that she literally couldn't carry them all. As she rode off all smiles, I went home once again to start my vigil by the phone.

Thirty-two hours later she returned again, safe and

sound, full of stories and a little tummy ache. It seems that despite my lectures to the contrary, she still refused to use the latrine and hadn't gone to the bathroom since she left home the morning before! I'll never know how she survived!

Several weeks later, she went to another camp. (You'd think I'd learn!)

My first big surprise was when I started to clean her thermos the first afternoon, only to find that she had snuck a live minnow home in it!

Now, what do you do with a cherished minnow? I couldn't release it in our canal because this was a fresh water minnow on a salt restricted diet! I couldn't put it in regular tap water because of the chemicals. Before I knew it, I was running outside before and after each rain storm collecting water for the stupid minnow.

Then there was the problem of what to feed it. I gave it tiny pieces of lettuce, and carrot, and bread crumbs and raw meat. None of these were apparently too appealing. The minnow seemed to be on a hunger strike.

Finally I laid down the law. The minnow had to go. Reluctantly, my daughter agreed. But how does one dispose of a minnow? After much discussion and a few tears, she finally snuck it back on the bus and back to camp in a jar in her lunch box.

But the final straw came on a day when the campers traditionally do not take bathing suits and go to a movie and then visit a park or local attraction instead. She had had to miss camp the Monday and Tuesday before that so we just assumed that this Wednesday would be the same as any other.

But, when we arrived at the bus stop, there were all the other little kids sitting there quietly, all wearing or carrying their bathing suits.

"Didn't you know?" one of the kids asked, "We're going to the beach today after the movie."

I dropped my daughter off and raced home in the car to get her bathing suit and towel. Then I flew back to the bus stop to learn that it had come early and I had missed it.

In the back of my mind, I thought I remembered the next

place that the bus was to stop. Back in the car I hopped, stepped on the gas and drove a good 10 miles to the next stop, only to find out that that was the stop before ours, not after.

By this point, I was seething. Here I was, dressed in my grubbiest clothes because I had planned to go right home and clean the house, and now I would have to go traipsing all over Lee County hunting a missing bus.

I stopped at the pay phone to call camp headquarters but I didn't have the right change. When I finally found a phone I was told that the best place to meet them would be to go directly to the theater, some 25 minutes away!

So, an hour after I originally dropped her off at the bus stop, I finally caught up with my daughter as she was stepping off the bus.

"Here's your suit," I said. "Now enjoy your last few days at camp. After this, we're going to need a vacation!"

It's too soon to play the dating game

It's taken me a long time to get used to the fact that my 8-year-old daughter is growing up.

She's starting to choose her own clothes -- string bikinis and purple blouses -- and she spent her last allowance on a bottle of nail polish. I decided to chip in for a bottle of nail polish remover, just in case.

She likes to go to the store and buy something by herself, just like her mother. And her taste in music leans toward disco tunes I thought only influenced teenagers.

It was quite difficult for me to accept the fact that she can have phone conversations with her friends. I mean it was only yesterday that I was teaching her how to dial the phone. Now she can even look up a number in the phone book.

For years all the telephone calls have been for me or my husband. All of a sudden she seems to be getting more calls than anyone else in the house.

So when the telephone rang last week and she started talking, I didn't pay much attention. But then she put the phone down and ran over to ask me a question.

"Brian wants to know if I can go out to dinner with him," she beamed.

"Who's Brian?" I asked her in surprise.

Brian, it turned out, was a boy she had met at Y-camp this summer, and she had decided he was pretty neat.

"He's a great dancer, Mom," she said. "Can I go out with him, please?"

"Just hold on," I said on the verge of panic. Things were moving pretty quickly, and I hadn't planned to have this conversation for another three or four years. I just wasn't prepared.

"I think I better talk to his parents before we make any arrangements for your first date," I told her.

She was crushed. After all, an 8-year-old should be able to handle these things by herself. At least that's how she saw it.

But it didn't take long before I was telling Brian's father how to get to our house, and he was telling me what time they would pick up my daughter, and I was telling myself that life was going by entirely too quickly.

By the time Brian arrived to pick up my daughter, she was floating on a cloud. And when his father complimented his son on his "good taste," my daughter burst into a smile a mile wide, and they left.

I couldn't wait for her to get home. I can tell I'm in for a terrible motherhood, waiting at the door until they're all home every night.

Brian brought her to the door.

"Isn't he a real gentleman?" my daughter whispered.

"We sat at a table all by ourselves," she said excitedly.

"He even paid for my hamburger and fries," she said.

"And look at this nice little gift he bought me," she said, bubbling over with enthusiasm.

"Isn't he wonderful?" she said.

I just don't know what to think. My "How To Raise a Happy Child" book doesn't have a chapter on dating, but I remember my own dating days all too well.

And that's why I've decided not to let anyone answer the phone at our house for the next 12 years. By that time I'll be old enough to have forgotten what dates are really like. Then it's my daughter's problem.

Take the bike
and leave the worrying to us

Do you remember several years ago when the federal government spent thousands of dollars to find out why little children fall off tricycles? It was in the news quite a bit.

I could have saved them a lot of money if they would have come to me with the question. My daughter used to fall off her trike regularly. All the kids in the neighborhood did. It's something we mothers learn to accept. But nobody asked me, so the government spent their money and I kept my mouth shut.

I saw a news story the other day about something that reminded me of the tricycle study. And I just started chuckling all over again.

It seems that at the Biomechanics Laboratory at Pennsylvania State University they're pioneering research on the bicycle. And early research has produced some interesting findings.

• Most bike riders subconsciously overuse one leg, though it's not the same leg each ride. While most riders are sure that they use each leg equally, some use one leg up to 40 percent more than the other.

• We all have an "optimum seat height." That means we are wasting energy if the seat is too high or too low for our bodies. Few know their correct seat height.

• The long-advocated "ankling" technique of bike-riding (dropping the heel on the pedal) is not the most efficient way of riding a bike, even though most experts swear by it. In fact the opposite foot alignment (dropping the toe on the pedal) is more common among experienced cyclists.

Why bicycle research? Well, for years there was no real safety or performance standards for bicycles, according to

69

the laboratory. But because of the recent bike boom, the Consumer Product Safety Commission and the National Bureau of Standards have decided that more information on bicycles is necessary.

I tried to tell my daughter about the latest research on bicycles the other day. The timing couldn't have been better. She just got a new bike for her birthday. It has three speeds, handbrakes and a fancy seat and she thinks she's the hottest thing on wheels.

Well, I decided to impart my new knowledge on bicycles as she was taking her first ride on her new bike.

"Don't overuse one leg," I yelled. "You're probably subconsciously overusing one leg!"

"What?" she said, as she turned to look at me and ran into the bush near our driveway.

"Mommy, what are you talking about?" she asked, as she looked up at me from the ground.

I assured her that it was nothing important, as I tried to measure her optimum seat height.

She wanted the seat closer to the ground, but I told her that research proved she was wasting too much energy and that her seat should be higher, even though she didn't know her optimum seat height.

She got on the bike again, barely able to reach the pedals, and took off. Even research doesn't alter a kid's enthusiasm for a new bike.

"You're ankling," I yelled as she rode up the street. "Don't ankle, use the opposite foot alignment. Drop your toe on the pedal!"

She looked back at me with a puzzled expression, as she careened from one side of the street to the other. "What are you talking about, Mommy? Are you crazy?" she said.

I shut my eyes as she ran off the side of the road and tumbled onto someone's front yard. "Never mind," I yelled. "The heck with this research."

I guess if she survived the tricycle, she can survive the bicycle, too.

My daughter's skates go faster
than mine ever did

I thought it would be fun to get my daughter roller skates.
What a mistake!

She loves them. I hate them.

They've added hours to her playtime. They've taken
years off my life.

Watching your child putting on her first pair of roller
skates is like riding on the roller coaster for the first time --
the anticipation is a killer. But as she flashed by me at
nearly the speed of sound, all I saw was the sparkle of her
smile.

In no time at all she was off and rolling like a professional
skater.

"Slow down," I yelled as she left the garage and started
down the driveway.

"I'm not going too fast," she shouted back. I nearly
suffered whiplash just watching her.

When she got to the end of the driveway, I could see the
catastrophic finale coming to her first attempt at skating.

"How do you turn around!" she yelled over her shoulder.
"Oh, never mind. I know how." With that she simply sat
down and let her rear end do the rest. What an emergency
brake!

Things were up hill from there. For her, at least. For
me, things have gotten worse.

Everytime I see her lacing up those skates, my stomach
starts to tie itself up in knots. It's not that I'm a nervous
mother. It's just that she skates like a bull in a china shop,
going from object to object and hitting them all with full
force.

If the car is in the driveway, she'll collide with it. If the
garage door is closed, she'll slam into it. If the bike is in the
driveway, she'll fall over it. She's taken more tumbles in
the past week than the clothes in my dryer.

So when I noticed an article on safety tips for roller
skaters last week, I read every word and then clipped it out
and put it on my daughter's bed.

71

"Oh, mother," she said later. "You don't think I'm going to wear safety pads on my knees and elbows, do you."

The fact that there were more than 100,000 skaters who landed up in the hospital emergency rooms last year didn't faze her a bit.

"I'm not going to wear a helmet! I'm not going to wear gloves! And I'm not going to wear a mouthpiece," she said.

She's right, of course. Only a parent or a dentist would wear a mouthpiece while roller skating. But it sounded like a good idea at the time.

When I think back on my own childhood, which is getting farther behind me than I care to realize, I remember roller skating down the sidewalk without a worry in the world. None of my friends wore knee pads or helmets, and mouthpieces were for boxers.

But the equipment has changed a lot since then. And so has the speed.

My roller skates were the metal kind that clipped onto a pair of leather shoes. My mother may have been worrying about broken arms and knocked-out teeth, but the only thing I worried about was not losing the roller skate key. I did lose it regularly, by the way.

My daughter's skates don't even remotely resemble my old skates. Hers are shoe skates made out of fancy white leather with red stripes. And the wheels are made of plastic, not metal. They sound like a finely-tuned sports car, compared to my old clip-ons.

And her skates seem to go much faster than mine did when I was a child. But then, life seems to go much faster, too.

7

Marriage is
a million laughs

Money is a taxing problem

Tax time is trouble time at our house. Each year it's the same story, and this year was no different.

Right around Christmas time, when the money is going out faster than it's coming in, I usually inquire about the income tax.

"Let's do our taxes early this year so we won't have to worry about it," I say sweetly. My husband usually says something like "the 1040 forms aren't even here yet."

The day the tax forms arrive, I say "Guess what came in the mail today, dear. The 1040 forms for our income tax. Maybe we could send them in early this year."

He invariably says, "We don't have all the figures we need. When they come, I can get to work on the taxes."

By the end of January I always issue a gentle reminder, "The dividend statements came two weeks ago, and the interest from the bank account is all on this little statement. Why don't we figure out our taxes and get them in early this year?"

He always has a good excuse. The W-2 forms aren't out yet, or the bank hasn't figured out the interest on the mortgage, or we haven't received an interest statement from some trust fund. By the end of January there is always something that is still missing.

Then most of February he spends debating whether to send the taxes to some accountant or do them himself.

During the first three weeks in March we search the house for any stray medical receipts or other records that are vital to tax preparation.

Then in late March he gets down to business.

Laying out all the records is an elaborate procedure. It takes the dining room table (with the extension leaves in) and half of the living room. Stacks of cancelled checks are piled up in front of the sofa. Medical receipts and insurance papers are spread out in front of the stereo. Extra forms from the IRS take up one corner of the living room while booklets containing hints on taxes are spread out over the coffee table. On the dining room table are a calculator, three legal pads, a jar full of freshly sharpened pencils and two new erasers.

The first task is to go through the cancelled checks to see if they all match up with the medical bills.

"Did you write a check for your visit to the doctor on May 5?" he asks. How do I know. That was nearly a year ago.

"I've got a cancelled check for the kids' dentists, but no copy of any bill. Was that for one or two visits?" he asks.

And on it goes for several nights as he sorts through a year's worth of bills and receipts.

"Why don't you keep better records of your expenses?" he says with a frown.

"Me!' You're the one who scatters this stuff all over the house," I say defiantly.

"Well, if you would keep these things in order, I wouldn't have to search through all this mess," he retorts.

"If you'd make room for some place to keep these bills and receipts, then I could keep them in order," I yell.

By this time the kids sense a beauty of a fight, and my husband decides to go to bed and do the taxes the next day. For five days nobody can walk in the dining room or living room for fear of messing up "his system."

Finally by the first of April, he is ready to start putting figures down on paper. Every year he gets about half way through schedule A and comes up with an unsolvable problem that he has to seek advice on from the IRS toll-free number. Now naturally, the toll-free number is either busy or not in operation after dinner time. So the big question of whether we owe or we get back money is delayed for another day.

After he gets the right advice (or the wrong advice) he

is finally ready for the big total. I spend three solid months worrying about whether we will owe the government more money and he has to double check everything before he will tell me the answer.

When we were all through last year, he brought home a large accordian folder and announced that we were going to keep all possible tax records in the folder as we collected them this year. That way it wouldn't be such a hassle next year.

That's a great idea. Now if I could just remember where I put the receipt from the visit to the dentist in January.

Just one mower problem

I can't begin to tell you how much fun has gone out of my life since we made the big move to Florida and bought a new lawn mower.

Some people like sports, others like cards, but one of my favorite pastimes used to be sitting in the house watching the all-out war that would take place each week as my husband attempted to cut the grass.

You see, my husband is perhaps the nicest, gentlest, most mild-mannered man I've ever met. As long as I've known him he has had only one mortal enemy-- his old lawn mower. I'm telling you, that lawn mower was almost human and the two of them were arch enemies. It was hysterical.

That old red devil entered our lives shortly after our marriage as a present from my in-laws. It was a real classy mower in its day -- one of those fancy self-propelled jobs with a grass catcher -- and oh, was he thrilled to get it.

The trouble began almost immediately. The darn thing wouldn't start. Although it was supposed to start up immediately with one quick pull on the cord, that fiesty machine wouldn't budge. It was then that it made the first trip to the friendly repair man.

A week later my husband went to the repair shop to pick it up.

"I'll tell you the truth, sir, I couldn't find one thing wrong with it. I tried to start it four or five times and each time it worked perfectly. It's a beauty. Maybe you're not doing it right. Let me watch you one time."

My husband pulled the cord just like he always did. It worked like a charm! He muttered something under his breath, thanked the man, and brought the mower home.

Once home we went out into the yard to start it up again. Nothing. He gave it another pull. Nothing. He pulled and pulled and yanked and yanked. Nothing.

The first time we both found it terribly amusing. After 15 tries I had tears streaming down my face trying to hold back the laughter. My husband's face, on the other hand, was red with rage. It was the first time I had ever heard him curse. Then, on the 18th try, it started right up and it worked perfectly the rest of the day.

Week after week the same thing would happen and my poor husband would get madder and madder. Each week it would take longer to start it and after a month or so my husband started to hit it and shove it in retaliation!

By this time I suggested we try another repair man. We did.

"This is really a beautiful lawn mower," he said to my husband when he went to pick it up. "I just made some minor adjustments and it works just fine," he said.

But once back home the same thing happened, only by this time the word had spread and a lot of our neighborhood friends had come down to watch him start the lawn mower. The more we'd laugh the worse it got and if the mower hadn't weighed so much, I'm sure he would have picked the thing up and thrown it across the yard.

By this time it was taking him anywhere from 20 to 40 tries to start it. My husband was seriously thinking of selling it and mentioned this to the repair man on one of our many visits.

"Sir, you shouldn't sell it. This is an excellent lawn mower and besides, it's putting food on my table," he laughed.

"But it hates me," my husband tried to explain.

Over the years things went from bad to worse. Not only

would the mower not start, but once it did it would soon stall out!

One night my husband had had it. He had been trying to cut the grass for well over two hours and our small yard was only half done. Suddenly it stalled again. My husband went wild. He called the thing every name in the book, shoved it as hard as he could and finished it off with a good swift kick! Then he reached down to start it again and away it went on the very first try.

Oh, did my husband feel good. At last he had won one.

"I guess you just have to show it who's boss," he yelled to me proudly as I stood in the doorway. Just then the mower made a loud, terrible sound and I saw my husband fall to the ground holding his leg. Believe it or not, that mower had blown a gasket or something with such force that it went through the red plastic casing and hit my husband on the leg!

That was it. He had the machine repaired but from then on he paid the boy up the street to bring his own lawn mower and cut our yard.

When we found out we were moving to Florida, one of the first thoughts my husband had was about the grass.

"How often do you have to cut it," he asked my father who lives here.

"About two or three times a week in the summer," he replied. My husband's face went pale.

"How much does it cost to have someone cut it?"

"Fifty dollars or more a month!"

That did it. Right then and there it was decided that our first priority after a house would be a new lawn mower with an automatic start.

"It'll be a good investment," he reasoned.

"Just eliminating all those aggravations should add five years to my life."

Well he got it and he was right. He may be the only man in Florida who can be seen cutting his grass in the 90 degree heat with a big smile on his face.

That new electric-start mower really lights up his life, but I still yearn for the good old days.

Keeping the bushes trim

Give a man a pair of pruning shears and he automatically turns into a butcher.

Why is it that my husband feels he has to scalp the shrubbery at least four times a year?

Whack, whack, whack!

He just took advantage of a three-day weekend to get "a little gardening done." Now our yard looks like the aftermath of a forest fire. All that is left is a bunch of brown, stubby trunks with a few twigs and branches. There's not a green leaf in sight. And of course the brown lawn that hasn't been watered for weeks lends some authenticity to the scene.

Whack, whack, whack!

I tremble every time he picks up a pair of hedge clippers. He just doesn't know when to stop.

My husband has abandoned the electric hedge trimmer I bought for his birthday one year. He claims it can't cut as well as the hand-powered model. Actually, the electric clippers continually jam up when he tries to cut through those inch-thick branches.

Whack, whack, whack!

He can take a beautiful, leafy hibiscus bush and reduce it to the size of a marigold in just a matter of minutes. And it does no good to protest.

"You don't want this plant to be tall and stringy, do you," he asks with that quizzical look. "If we trim it back now, it will be nice and bushy and blooming in no time at all."

Whack, whack, whack!

Whenever we buy a new plant or shrub, the first thing he does is trim it. For the life of me, I can't figure out why we look for the largest plant at the nursery and then trim it back to the size of all the plants we passed up.

But he claims it will become bushier, have better roots, and be a better plant despite the trauma of the slaughter.

Whack, whack, whack!

He's standing in the front yard, looking at the two-year-old tree that is my prized possession.

"If we trim these three lower branches, the tree will have a better shape, and will grow a lot faster," he says, clippers in hand.

I've been waiting for this moment. I've got all my arguments ready: we need a tree with low branches so the kids can climb; the low branches hide the view of the vacant lot across the street; let's leave Mother Nature alone so she can create her own wonders.

But my husband points out that by the time the tree is strong enough for the kids to climb on, the kids will be too tall for the lower branches. And the vacant lot across the street won't be vacant forever. And Mother Nature needs a helping hand now and then. Besides, it's too hard to mow the grass around a tree with so many low branches.

Whack, whack, whack!

I've noticed that no matter what the season, he's always got a valid reason for amputating the shrubbery. In the summer, the rain will make the plants grow back in no time. In the winter, they need to be trimmed back for spring. It goes on and on.

But no matter what time of year it is, we always end up in an argument over the pruning.

When we're having out-of-town guests, I hide the clippers, the pruning shears and the hedge trimmers at least a month in advance of their visit.

And when I see him taking an inspection tour of the yard I usually bring the kids inside. The tour usually ends in a trimming, and if I don't get the kids in the house, they're liable to get a free haircut to boot!

Maybe that's the problem. Maybe my husband is just a frustrated barber, taking it out on our shrubbery.

Whack, whack, whack!

"Why are there ladybugs in my refrigerator?"

Did you ever have a craving for something so bad that you were willing to do almost anything to get it?

Well, last week I was so up for some delicious fresh-from-the-garden vegetables that I almost broke down and decided to throw caution to the wind and plunge wholeheartedly into a new vegetable garden.

But just in the nick of time I remembered our disastrous track record and the voice of reason got a hold of me.

I figured agriculturally, Florida was having enough problems with its sugar cane blight and it's hoards of insects. It just wasn't fair to subject it to my string of bad luck.

It all started shortly after we were married when we bought our first little house with a nice big back yard with plenty of room for our first little vegetable garden.

That year organic gardening was just starting to be a big thing and many people were touting the practice of fighting Japanese beetles and other insects damaging to crops with other insects rather than chemical sprays. My husband thought that was about the best idea he had ever heard, so without mentioning it to me, he put in his order forthwith.

Several weeks later the mailman arrived asking me to sign for two very interesting looking parcels. My birthday was only several days away and since no one was around, I didn't think it would hurt if I had a little sneak preview of what was to come, so I peeked in the boxes.

Well, had a large mouse jumped out at me I couldn't have been more startled. There in those boxes were 50 praying mantises and 1,000 lady bugs!

I thought I was going to die of a heart attack right on the spot. I phoned my husband at work immediately to give him a piece of my mind.

"What are you going to do with them?" I demanded. "If we put all these things in our yard I'll be afraid to walk out the door."

"Now calm down honey, you don't understand," my

husband said soothingly. "You don't put them out there all at once. You put them in the refrigerator to keep them dormant. Then when you need them you take a few out at night and put them in your garden. The next morning when the heat awakens them they will be so ravenously hungry they'll eat all the other bugs in sight!"

If you think I was mad before, you should have seen me then. I am one of those people who is afraid of any and all insects and the thought of keeping them in my refrigerator made my skin crawl!

Finally we arrived at a compromise. I agreed to let the ladybugs sleep in my 'fridge' but the praying mantises would have to be released immediately that night.

Believe it or not it worked pretty well and our little garden grew and grew. Soon we would be able to taste the fruits of our labor. We could hardly wait.

Unfortunately, wild onions were flourishing in our beautiful yard as well, and every time my husband cut the grass our whole yard would smell like onion breath! It was disgusting.

We took our problem to the garden center and returned home with some poisonous powder that, when dusted on our yard, would kill the wild onions and leave the grass. Pretty clever. Our problem would soon be solved.

We followed the instructions to a T and sprinkled the stuff on our lawn. We never gave a thought to the slight breeze that night.

The next morning we woke up and were aghast. Not only had the stuff killed our wild onions, but it had blown over and killed everything in our vegetable garden as well!

That ended our gardening in West Virginia.

Several years later we were living in Western New York. There, city officials rented out small garden plots for $1 a season to anyone who didn't have room to plant a garden in their own yard. The soil was terrific. The price was right. And it seemed to be the thing to do. So once again we took the plunge!

At the end of May we received our plot assignment by mail. We rushed down to the garden and although the boundaries of the plots were poorly marked we counted them out, found the one that had to be ours, and staked our claim. While I went out shopping for chicken wire, wooden stakes, seeds and plants, my husband went to work weeding his garden. He spent all weekend, dawn to dusk, weeding that thing but when he was done, it was beautiful. We planted our seeds and, filled with contentment, sat back to watch nature take its course.

But on Monday, the agricultural extension agent phoned. He had some bad news for us. We had accidentally farmed the plot adjacent to the one we had actually been assigned and, rather than switch, the man who was really assigned that plot was claiming it as his! The agent apologized profusely and said he tried hard to make the man switch plots but he wouldn't, so there was nothing else that could be done. We could take back our chicken wire and stakes, but we'd have to start over!

What a blow. My husband was simply defeated. He had worked so hard and didn't have the time or the inclination to do it all again. I felt so sorry for him. (If I had only saved my deadly dust I would have paid a midnight visit to our neighboring garden plot!) But alas, we had no revenge.

After waiting a week or two, we finally broke down and did a little planting in our plot -- a few tomatoes, some lettuce, carrots, corn and zucchini. It wasn't nearly as nice as the first one. We just didn't have the enthusiasm any more.

But when our friends started coming home with things from their gardens we felt a renewed interest. We returned to our plot. Not having thought about rotating our crops, we found we had 50 to 100 heads of lettuce all ready at the same time!

And the zucchini! Whosh! I've since decided that zucchini must be the rabbits of the vegetable world! They multiply like mad! We'd have zucchini bread for breakfast and fried zucchini for dinner. And we couldn't even give them away because everyone we knew was loaded with them too!

The raccoons ate all our corn -- we didn't even get one ear -- and just about the time our tomatoes were ready New

York had its first frost. Then someone stole our chicken wire and stakes!

Once again it was a disaster. We vowed at that moment never again to try to compete with the jolly green giant. For some reason, it's just not in the cards.

8

Where did they put the basement?

A model house is not a home

When I need a boost or want to beat the blahs, the outrageous model homes really give me guffaws.

The designs are wild. The decorations wacky. And some of these famous showcases are downright tacky!

I guess I just don't go into these models with the right frame of mind.

When I gaze upon a sofa with only half a back perched on a second-story loft, I can just see myself sitting back to relax after an exhausting day with the kids and doing a back flip in tuck position down to the first floor.

And when I see a loft in a youngster's bedroom, I immediately picture my daughter getting up in the middle of the night, walking in her sleep and plunging head first through the canopy below!

Another fascinating thing about these model homes and condos is the use of white carpets and white walls. Talk about nerve!

Why, just one gooky peanut butter and jelly sandwich, one spilled glass of grape juice, or one hated piece of tomato thrown defiantly from the highchair and those apartments would take on a little color in no time. And when your darling little kitty or puppy tracks dirty little paw marks all over the place, you could just tell your friends that you have bought the very latest in animal prints!

Have you seen how they decorate a child's bedroom in the models? White furniture, Nettle Creek bedspread, one small toy box shaped like a circus wagon, and a few plants. Let's face reality, shall we. The day I put a Nettle Creek spread on my kid's bed is the day I finally flip out. And the toy chest! We've got two closets full of toys and they're still flowing out into the hallway.

The master bedrooms, on the other hand, are a story in themselves. Why, I never realized how dull my sexlife must be until I took up the hobby of touring model homes.

What a show! Bathtubs for two backed by mirrors, flanked by white columns, and topped by a gold and crystal chandelier...fancy bedrooms with round beds...or mirrored ceilings...glassed-in showers in the midst of a private garden.

Why, some of the boudoirs in these places look like the perfect setting for a book entitled "The Sensual Couple." It's downright shocking! Just picturing a little old couple from the midwest retiring to Florida in a house like that is enough to keep me smiling for hours.

Even more fun than touring these rooms yourself is standing back quietly in a corner and watching the reactions of other people. Raised eyebrows...a quiet smirk...wide-eyed wonder...or outright laughter says it all.

It's rooms like these that really make you wonder about the priorities of the builder. Some homes have tiny living rooms with little or no dining area but bathrooms and closets bigger than some of my bedrooms!

And the pools! There are big pools, little pools, pools you can eat in, pools with statues, pools with fountains and pools with waterfalls. In fact one model boasts two outdoor pools and an indoor bathtub that's bigger than my daughter's wading pool. Why, it would cost you a fortune in water every time you took a bath.

But the saunas are the things that really get me. The way I look at it, Florida is one big sauna! All you have to do is walk outside and spend five minutes or so in this unbelievably hot sun and you'll be sweating like mad. And it doesn't even cost a dime. Just one of the benefits of Florida living.

Another thing I marvel at is the kitchen counter space. Of course, I haven't seen my own kitchen counter in months. I know it's under all of the newspapers, the lunchbox, the boxes of cereal and the grocery coupons, but I've frankly forgotten what color it is.

The kitchens in the model homes are a different story. The only thing gracing the countertops is an occasional plastic piece of cheese or a plaster-of-paris loaf of bread. There are no rotting brown bananas on top of the refrigerator, no school lunch menus taped to the front of the refrigerator and no sticky Kool-Aid running down the side of the refrigerator. It's the refrigerator of my dreams.

What I like, however, is the pure entertainment of all of it. Rome may have its Colosseum, Paris its Eiffel Tower, and New York the Statue of Liberty. But Southwest Florida has model homes, and that's some of the best entertainment of all.

But after a few hours of searching for the latest in building and decorating, I'm always happy to get back to my own hacienda. After all, a model house is not a home, you know.

In the heat of the night ...

"Let's do it today," I pleaded.

"Just wait a few more days," my husband said.

"I can't wait any longer. Let's do it," I begged.

"Not yet. Hold off until the weekend," he said.

"That's three more days, and I just can't wait that long," I implored.

"You're going to have to wait," he said.

If this conversation sounds a bit strange to you, it is an annual occurrence in our house. Every year in May we go through the battle of the air conditioner.

I'm all for turning on the switch at the first sign of heat, but my husband tries to hold off until it gets unbearably hot.

You see, I'm one of those un-patriotic Americans who believes that the temperature around me should be as comfortable as possible. We have the technological knowledge to make it cool, so why should we sweat. We can make it warm, so why should we freeze?

I know that it's unfashionable at the moment, and I'm not against conservation of anything. But the heat in Florida is insufferable. And if it's possible to make my home a little cooler than the prevailing temperature, I want to take full advantage of the situation.

My husband, on the other hand, likes to go around the house calculating how much energy we save by turning off the night light and boiling water at a lower temperature.

It's not that he's so patriotic. It's just that he pays the bills. And when the size of the electric bill starts to equal the size of his paycheck, he starts to panic.

"You could get those clothes just as clean by washing them in cooler water," he says.

"If you're not going to sit in that corner, why don't you turn the light off?" he says.

"Why don't we unplug the clock in the guest room since there aren't any guests?" he says.

Does the refrigerator really need to be set at such a low temperature?" he asks, holding a warm glass of milk.

He even went so far as to suggest that we sell the clothes dryer and buy a clothes line. I must admit I got some smug satisfaction when my daughter asked him what a clothesline was.

But the biggest battle of the year clearly is the air conditioner. He resists turning it on until the only alternative is divorce.

His theory is that once the air conditioner is on, it isn't turned off until October. And each year he tries to push that date back earlier and earlier.

And throughout the summer months it is a constant battle over the thermostat controls. If I set the thermostat at 78 degrees, within five minutes he gets an exaggerated chill and turns it up to 82. Our thermostat goes back and forth more than a pendulum.

If he has been swimming in the pool and comes into the house dripping wet, he complains that the air conditioner is too low.

If he has been cutting the grass and comes into the house in a sweat, he says the temperature is too cool.

"Oh, God, not another beautiful day!"

If he wakes up at night and has to cover up with a sheet, he thinks the house is too cool.

My theory is simple: why sweat if you don't have to?

And until I live in a house that is designed for the climate, until I have a house with windows in the bedroom that I can leave open at night, we will continue to argue about the air conditioner.

I guess that's the price you pay for living in Florida. And the price is getting higher every year.

The ice man cometh

When we moved into our house three years ago I was delighted to find the refrigerator of my dreams.

You've probably seen the advertisements -- it dispenses ice cubes, crushed ice or ice water at the touch of a button. And all without opening the door to the freezer.

What visions I had. If my daughter and her friends were thirsty, I could point them in the direction of the refrigerator and they could get their own cold water. If we were having a party, we wouldn't even need an ice bucket. The guests could line up at the refrigerator. If I needed crushed ice for a thermos bottle, I wouldn't have to search through the attic for the ice crusher. All I would need to do was flip a switch on the refrigerator door.

Well, in the past three years my dream has turned into a nightmare. An expensive nightmare.

I think the first sign of trouble was when the ice maker decided not to make any ice. That's when I first met Harry, the Houdini of appliance repairs.

Harry took one look at the empty ice tray and announced that the problem was with the ice maker. Harry has a great sense of humor. That's the only reason he's still on my payroll.

He turned a few screws and tightened a few gaskets and my dream machine was soon churning out ice cubes again. That first visit only cost me $22. I was never that lucky again.

A few months later the refrigerator stopped spitting out ice cubes again. Harry said the motor was frozen.

"Frozen!" I yelled. "How could a motor in a freezer be frozen!"

He didn't know. He just borrowed my hair dryer, thawed out the motor, and presented me with a bill for $30.

The same thing happened again the following month. He brought his own hair dryer this time. I guess he thought he could charge more if he didn't use my equipment. And he pulled some of the insulation out from around the sides of the motor. His theory was simple: the motor was getting too warm, causing the ice to melt, and when the motor shut off, the ice froze in the motor. "That will be $35, please."

When it happened a third time, we began to search for another cause. And we soon realized that every time the electricity went off during a storm, the ice maker motor would freeze. By this time I knew how to thaw out the motor myself. So I saved $35.

But just when I had learned how to fix the ice maker, something else happened. The mechanism that deposits ice cubes in your glass suddenly started churning out only crushed ice.

Harry showed me the simple solution -- you have to pound the tray a few times to dislodge the switch. No real problem, just $30.

The next time the ice cubes stopped dropping out of the ice maker, I debated for a week about whether it was worth getting fixed. After all, a few trays of ice cubes couldn't be that much trouble. But some out-of-town guests were due to arrive for a week-long visit, and the thought of going a week without my marvelous ice maker made me shudder. So Harry came by again, changed a gasket and charged me $35.

When the hose leading to the ice maker broke and flooded the kitchen floor, Harry got a bonus -- $65. And when the refrigerator overheated, Harry sprayed the bottom of the machine with air and collected $35.

My problems with the refrigerator don't end with the repair bills. The kids think the ice water dispenser is one of man's greatest inventions. They bring kids from blocks away into the kitchen to witness the magic machine.

Of course every time they use the dispenser, the water either misses the glass and squirts all over the place, or they don't shut it off soon enough and the glass of water overflows. No matter which one happens, the water all ends up in the same place -- on the floor.

But enroute to the floor, it flows down the front of the refrigerator, which is now beginning to show spots of rust worse than my car. And of course the water on the floor does make for some slippery moments in front of the refrigerator.

"I'm thinking about getting a new refrigerator," I told Harry one day when he stopped by for coffee. "This machine is a lemon. It's nothing but trouble.

Harry just smiled. He knows me well enough by now to realize that I'm hooked on the cursed machine, that I couldn't give up my crushed ice.

"That's crazy," Harry said. "This refrigerator is the best you can buy. Besides, my son is only in his junior year in college. You've got to keep this refrigerator for another year until he graduates. How else can I afford the tuition?"

Rainy day blues

There's nothing worse than waking up on a weekend in Florida and hearing the pitter patter of raindrops on the windows. Oh, I'm sure there ARE worse things.

When I lived up North, rainy weekends were something I grew to expect. Like the flu in the winter and ants on picnics, rain on the weekends was a natural occurrence.

You learned not to promise the kids they could go to the zoo on Saturday because, more often than not, a rain cloud would drift over the area late Friday night and become "stationary" until Sunday evening. In fact "gray weekends" became somewhat of a joke and being trapped in the house was something you had to live with.

But here in Florida it is rare to have to cancel your weekend plans, and somehow you expect the Saturdays and Sundays of your life to be glorious. That's why it is such a downer to forego a trip to the beach or a ride on the boat. It's terrible to be trapped inside for two days in such an "outdoor-state."

Not that there isn't a lot to do inside. I thought of a lot of jobs around the house that needed to be done. But the rainy day blues got to me, and I found valid reasons not to do any of the things that I should have done.

Take house-cleaning for example. What better day to clean the house than a rainy day! But the job seemed so enormous that it was just too big to tackle. So I decided to focus in on a few specific jobs.

• Clean out the closet in my daughter's bedroom. That's something I've been meaning to do since last Christmas. She's got so many toys in that closet that there's hardly room for any clothes. I took one look and decided that job would be good practice for my daughter. After all, she may be a mother some day, and she should know about all the pitfalls early in life. Well, that's one task avoided.

• Polish the silver. The last time I looked, some of it had turned from silver to black. A rainy day is a perfect day to clean the silver, I thought as I went hunting for it. But when I found it I realized that more of the silver had tarnished than I remembered, and of course I didn't have enough silver polish. Besides, how often do you use silver down here anyway. Why waste the time?

• Put all the snapshots in the photo album. I always used to enjoy doing that up North, I thought, as I gathered the pictures that are scattered in various drawers throughout the house. In no time at all, I was holding about 300 snapshots, and I realized that I hadn't put a single picture in a photo album since we moved to Florida several years ago. And I didn't want to get all wet going to the store to buy five new photo albums for those snapshots, so I clicked that idea off my list.

• Straighten up all my cookbooks and file all my recipe cards. You see, I have one entire cabinet in the kitchen that I've been tossing recipes into since we moved in.

Everytime I read something that sounds good, I clip it and stuff it in a cookbook or put it on a shelf. What a mess! And whenever I try to find something, it takes me an hour to look through the cabinet. I took one look at all the clipped recipes and decided it would take more than a rainy weekend to get me to straighten that mess up.

• Balance my checkbook. That was my husband's suggestion. Fat chance!

• Bake bread. That was my daughter's suggestion. And I gave it serious consideration. But it was too hot and muggy to bake bread, and besides, I never unpacked the bread pans when we moved.

• Fill in all the information in my second daughter's baby book. What a great idea. I stopped keeping track of her accomplishments after her first tooth appeared. And I've always been worried that when she grows up and sees that her sister's baby book is an accurate account of her first four years, and that hers stops at four months, she would feel we didn't love her as much. But after trying to remember whether she started walking at Thanksgiving or Christmas, and whether her first word was "cookie" or "mama," I gave up and wrote a little note in the book that said: "You did all the right things at all the right times!" That's the end of that book.

• Finish that needlepoint pillow I haven't worked on for 18 months. I found the pillow, and I found the yarn, but I never found the needle, so I put that project aside for a cold winter day, if any ever comes along.

So where do you put the car?

One of the nice things about living in Florida is that you don't have to clean out the basement.

One of the terrible things about living in Florida is that you do have to clean out the garage. And cleaning out the basement pales in comparison to that chore.

The basement in our home up north was about five times the size of my garage down here. It was full of old bookcases, rusted patio furniture, boxes of over-used toys, trunks of family photos, and souvenirs of ten years of marriage.

Because of the size of the basement, it was possible, with a little maneuvering and a lot of imagination, to make it look fairly neat and clean in just a few hours. Besides, nobody ever saw the basement except my own family and the meter reader. And an occasional plumber. So it didn't really matter if it got a little messy now and then.

The garage in Florida, however, is a different story. Every time one of the kids leaves the garage door open, I suspect my neighbors are on the phone gossiping about the mess. They're the only kids on the block who have electric garage door openers on their bikes. They've been instructed to shut the door as soon as the rear wheel of their bike leaves the garage.

My garage is such a pit, I'm embarrassed to pull the car out except in the dark of night. I'd leave it parked in the driveway all the time, but my husband worked for three weekends carving out space in the garage for my car, and I feel obligated to squeeze it in each day.

Actually, my garage is no worse than most that I've seen in Florida. There's the standard garden tools propped up in one corner. And the fishing poles in another corner, right next to the lawnmower, the bookcase full of half-empty cans of paint, and the snowtreads (just in case we go back up North for Christmas).

Then one wall is lined with shelves, and on those shelves are all our worldly possessions. Three cartons full of Christmas ornaments are on the top level, along with the boxes of "good" china and crystal. I can't remember if we put them up high because they are used so seldom, or if we use them so seldom because they're too hard to reach.

On another level are the books I've saved in case we ever buy a house with book cases beside the fireplace. Those books are getting a little green, but so is the brass fireplace set I brought down South with me. If I ever do need the books and fireplace set, they will blend together beautifully.

Just below the green books are boxes of tools, painting

supplies and assorted nuts and bolts my husband has collected through the years. Those boxes haven't been touched since we moved in. I'm surprised they aren't on the top shelf, too.

On the fourth shelf are three boxes of pots and pans and other kitchen utensils I haven't used since my mother gave them to me eight years ago. I guess I'm saving them for my oldest daughter.

On that same shelf is a carton containing dozens of old National Geographics, the "last" issue of LIFE Magazine, newspaper clippings of Nixon's last days and Kennedy's funeral. If you think the fireplace set is green, you should see those once-yellow National Geographics.

Underneath the shelves are the old tables, ladders, chairs, a broken TV set, and everything else that "didn't fit" in our house. Add some bicycles, some riding toys, hoses and a pet guinea pig cage and you've got a real mess.

About every three months we have a family project -- clean out the garage. We each argue about what should be thrown away and what should be moved to the attic.

"Do we really need all those old flower vases?" someone will say, and I will agree to toss one or two away. "Do we really need this ironing board?" I ask each time, but the rest of the family thinks I should have more attachment to it, and the ironing board stays.

I've often thought it would be easier to have one giant garage sale and clean it out for good. But I just can't part with all that junk. It's the story of my life.

Sweeping the dirt into the vacuum

Our family has made two big purchases since we moved to Florida. There was a new boat, of course. I've told you all about that. But the boat shouldn't overshadow the really important new addition to our household -- a new vacuum cleaner.

To say that we have needed a new vacuum cleaner for

years would be an understatement. Our old cleaner was so old, it should be placed in Thomas Edison's museum.

We got it 11 years ago from my aunt and uncle. They were having a household sale, and nobody bought their vacuum cleaner. So they took pity on us, a poor newly-married couple, and gave it to us.

At the time it seemed like a gift from heaven. And it did a presentable job of keeping our carpet clean on those rare occasions when I actually used it. Of course in those days I had a full-time job, and therefore an excuse to let the cleaning slide a bit.

But then our first child arrived, and I developed a more intimate relationship with our vacuum cleaner. I began to recognize some of its short comings.

It was a canister-type cleaner, but one of the sections of the cleaning wand was missing, so I had to constantly stoop over when cleaning the carpets. I began to feel somewhat like the hunchback of Notre Dame.

Despite that little drawback, the cleaner had great suction power. But one year I used the vacuum to clean up after we took down the Christmas tree. The hose quickly filled up with dead pine needles and the suction was never the same after that. Every Christmas since then I have picked up dead pine needles by hand, one by one. Talk about the end-of-the-holiday blues!

My husband tried to clean out the vacuum hose with a coat hanger, but I swear there are still some old pine needles in there from 1972.

Somehow through the years little holes developed in the vacuum hose. I tried wrapping tape around the hose but that didn't work. Then I developed the ability to hold my left hand around the hose to keep air from rushing in through the holes, and steering the vacuum hose with my right hand.

I know you are probably wondering why I didn't just get a new hose. Well, I always considered that simple solution, but I just never got around to it. You know how you always think there's no sense in fixing something that old because you will be getting a new model any day. That's the way it's been for years!

Things changed drastically when we moved to Florida. I think our old vacuum didn't like picking up sand. Sand was something foreign to its heritage, and the old machine just balked at the job of cleaning it up.

At some point during the past year the machine just decided to retire. Suction was reduced so greatly that I had to get down on my hands and knees and slowly comb back and forth with the vacuum hose, hoping against hope that it would pick up some of the bigger pieces of dirt. I vacuumed the carpet less and less frequently. Even the kids started complaining. My daughter started wearing shoes around the house so she wouldn't have to step on all the debris the vacuum cleaner refused to swallow.

The low point, though, was when a vacuum cleaner sales person happened to stop at my door one day to demonstrate his super-duper machine. When he looked at my antique vacuum, he just laughed.

His cleaner cleaned circles around mine -- literally! He picked up more dirt from my carpet in one minute than my cleaner had picked up in the whole year. I encouraged him to demonstrate his machine in every room of the house. Our carpet suddenly took on new color.

The sales person had a hard time accepting the fact that we wouldn't buy his product. It was obvious that we needed it. But when my husband looked at the price, he just laughed.

Ever since that day I have been searching for a new vacuum cleaner. I finally found one that did a good job and at the same time didn't clean out my pocketbook.

So now, for the first time in my life, I can clean the carpet without getting a backache. In fact, my new vacuum cleaner even has some sort of mechanism that makes it move by itself. Imagine that. I don't even have to push it. Almost like having a maid isn't it? Vacuuming can be fun!

By the way, we're going to hang onto our old cleaner. You never can tell. The historical society may pay me a good price for it some day!

9

Who said TV is
a vast wasteland?

"The Days of Our Lives" are nothing like mine

I don't know about the rest of you, but these soap operas just kill me.

I know they are supposed to make me feel good about my life after seeing all the monumental trials and tribulations they go through every day. But every day when I turn them off I'm so green with envy I'm ready to pack my bags and move immediately into my television set.

Face it. Those girls have it knocked!

How many of them do you see running around in a pair of holey pajamas with their hair in rollers changing dirty diapers and worrying about ring around the collar?

No. These broads lounge around their immaculate beautiful homes eating bon bons, wearing their latest Paris originals, waiting for their husbands to come home from a rough day at the office and sweep them off their feet and carry them into bed!

They make me sick!

What do they know about frizzy hair, middle age spread or the rise of inflation? These girls are all five feet ten, weigh 100 pounds, have gorgeous hair, flawless complexions and are married to either doctors, lawyers or business executives. They wouldn't know a pimple if they saw one.

Come to think of it, it's no wonder all those handsome men want to take them off to bed. I mean, have you seen those things they wear to go to sleep in? Woosh! Feathery flowing gowns, flimsy little nighties and strategically wrapped towels are a lot more enticing than my flannel granny gown.

Even their illnesses are exciting.

These people never have a common cold or hay fever or a wart on their toe.

They suffer from such things as convenient amnesia, dual personalities, operable brain tumors and non-fatal gunshot wounds almost as often as I get a sore throat. And they always survive! Paralysis is always temporary, heart attacks are usually minor and those with drinking problems can kick the habit in no time.

And while they're in the hospital they even have it made. Half the patients in the hospitals are either friends or relatives and they are given almost constant care by a dedicated staff of voluptuous nurses and absolutely gorgeous doctors.

Face it, these people on the soaps just don't know what it is to be bored. They know the juicy racy tidbits in everybody's past, and when they get together to discuss foreign affairs they're usually discussing the love life of the neighbor on the block.

And what really amazes me is that despite the countless mad passionate love affairs they have, very few of them ever have babies. They don't have little toddlers running about smearing a whole jar of cream deodorant all over the toilet seats and strewing rolls of toilet paper or paper towels throughout the house.

And the children they do have never bite their nails or pick their nose, or talk back, or climb all over them while they are trying to have a quiet and relaxing drink with their husbands before dinner. Heck no. They're too busy sitting in the corner reading silently with their hands folded neatly in their laps!

I don't know where I've gone wrong. Sometimes I swear there is more tension at our house some nights when I'm trying to prepare dinner than there was in Washington while Jimmy Carter tried to prepare the Mideast Peace Treaty.

One day I pondered the idea of putting the kids to bed early, buying a sexy black nightie and meeting my husband at the door with a big kiss and an extra-dry martini. But thank heaven I quickly changed my mind. He'd probably have a heart attack right on the spot, but unlike the soap operas, it would probably be fatal!

The grass is always greener in Dallas

I've never been to Dallas, but I know just what life is like down there.

Everyone lives on something called a ranch. A ranch is a huge white-columned mansion surrounded by miles of empty land. The land is used for growing cattle, horses and oil wells.

The people who live on these ranches all drive fancy cars and wear clothes that look like they belong in New York City. Except for the cowboy hats, that is.

They have servants that serve them meals, and ranch hands that serve them a little spice. They have secretaries that don't have to worry about taking dictation, and politicians who do.

How do I know about all of this?

Why am I such an expert on Dallas?

Because I watch it every Friday night on television. "Dallas" is that sordid serial that pits Texas oilmen against the rest of the world, and their own families, every Friday night on CBS.

The stars of the show are the Ewing family, a conglomerate of the good, the bad, and the beautiful. They are wealthy, wicked and wanton, just the thing to brighten up my Friday nights.

The worst of the bunch is J.R. Ewing, whose lust for money, power and women makes Attila the Hun look like a good guy. J.R. runs the family oil business, along with the rest of Texas. J.R. won't be happy until he destroys everyone who has a better reputation than his. And that's almost everyone on the show.

J.R.'s wife (if she is still his wife when you read this) is

Sue Ellen, a former beauty queen possessed with all the charm of Snow White's stepmother. Sue Ellen has shared beds with about as many men as J.R. has with women. They make a lovely couple.

Sue Ellen has a son. For a while we thought the father was Cliff Barnes, J.R.'s arch enemy who is doing everything he can to destroy the Ewing family once and for all. But later we found out that J.R. was actually the father. If this is getting confusing, you haven't heard anything yet.

Cliff's sister, the beautiful and sweet Pam, is married to J.R.'s brother, Bobby. They used to love each other, but now they are beginning to hate each other because they both want a child, but Pam is afraid to get pregnant because ... well, it's too involved to explain here.

They all live in a big white house on Southfork, their ranch that takes up about a quarter of Texas but which is conveniently located just minutes from downtown Dallas.

With them at Southfork are their mamma and daddy, Miss Ellie and Jock. They are a nice couple, prone to arguing a lot. But with their problems, who wouldn't?

In addition to their two sons and their wives, Miss Ellie and Jock also have their granddaughter (from another son) living with them. Her name is Lucy, but it should be Lolita. I went to school with a few "Lucys" myself, but they didn't talk with her Texas twang.

Every morning most of the family members gather by the pool for breakfast. They talk about their jobs, they talk about their problems, but mostly they talk about themselves.

After breakfast they each hop into their individual luxury cars and head for Dallas. You can tell they're in the oil business. They never even think about car pooling, even though they all go to the same place. Of course given the choice, I wouldn't want to ride with any one of them either.

J.R. works at Ewing Oil Co. He manipulates, maneuvers and manages the family's "holdings." He also molests his secretary, if you could call her that. In fact, J.R. is a regular Machiavelli.

Bobby sometimes works at Ewing Oil, and sometimes

works at Ewing ranch. Wherever he is working, however, he doesn't do much work. Instead, he worries about Pam's work.

Pam works at "The Store." I've always wondered if "The Store" is the name of the store, or if there is only one store in Texas worth mentioning, and that is **the store.**

Sue Ellen doesn't work. She goes to club meetings, charity luncheons, psychiatric sessions, and liaisons with male friends. Whenever she goes to lunch, she always goes to the Cattlemen's Club. In fact, everyone in Dallas always goes to the Cattlemen's Club for lunch.

After work, everyone heads back to Southfork. Well, not everyone. J.R. usually has dinner with his secretary, who incidentally is Sue Ellen's sister, and dinner sometimes extends into other things, if you know what I mean.

Sue Ellen often misses dinner at Southfork, too, when she has more exciting offers. And Pam sometimes has to work late at "The Store." So Bobby has dinner with old girl friends.

But it's better off, that way. Can you imagine all those people at the same table every night. No house in the world is big enough for their family.

No matter whether it's in the board room or the bedroom, "Dallas" has got to be the most exciting place in the world to live. No wonder all those oil companies are headquartered there. Those high rollers can afford the best, and they know Dallas is the place to find life at its most entertaining.

It's comforting to know that the Texas oilmen who will control our energy for the next few decades have so much energy of their own. They've got to have energy to live in Dallas. It's never boring. All the boring people move to Knots Landing, Calif. But that's another story.

10

How long do you wait on hold?

Has anyone seen the tape?

"Where's the Scotch tape?"

That was the question my daughter asked last week that launched a house-wide search. She was wrapping a present and when the time came to tape the present shut, there was no tape to be found.

"Why don't you just use some Bandaids," my husband said after 25 minutes of hunting for the tape.

"Daddy, that would look silly. This has to look like a nice present," she said in exasperation.

I found a roll of adhesive bandage and carefully put it in an obvious place where she could see it, but my daughter evidently thought that strips of white adhesive tape wouldn't go too well on pink flowered wrapping paper.

We checked every drawer and cupboard in the house, to no avail.

"The last time I used it, I put it in the desk drawer," my husband said.

"Well, I saw it in the bathroom drawer last week," I chimed in.

"My little sister probably threw it in the garbage," my daughter said.

After two hours, we finally gave up and went to the store to buy another roll of tape. But while I was searching the house, I started thinking about how certain things are never in the right place in our house.

Like glue. The glue bottle belongs in the kitchen cupboard, but do you think it's ever there when you want it?

Noooooo. No. It may be in the garage, or the bathroom, or the kids' toy chest, but not in the kitchen cupboard.

How many times have you been in the middle of a project, and when the critical point of making contact with something occurs, you can't find the glue? If it has never happened to you, then you must not have kids!

Another thing that's always missing is the nail clipper. Even though we must have three nail clippers in our house, when you really need one, it's impossible to find any of them.

Or how about a sharp pencil? Or a pencil with an eraser. I know there must be several hundred pencils with at least a stub of eraser hidden somewhere in our house, but when I want to write something down, or even worse, erase something, can I find one lousy pencil? No!

Extension cords are another item that seems to disappear. We can't find one at Christmas to plug the tree lights into. We can't find one in the summer to plug the electric fan into. We can't find one for the flood lights when it's time to take home movies. It's worse than the energy shortage.

Another elusive item at our house is the flashlight. But even worse are the batteries for the flashlight. Did we put the batteries in the camera flash unit, or the portable radio, or the electronic television game, or the toy train, or the digital electric scale? I know you're probably saying "why doesn't she just buy more batteries." But that's the problem. I've bought plenty of batteries over the years. They just aren't around when I need them.

An item doesn't have to be tiny to be misplaced. There are weeks when I can't locate the phone book, or the dictionary, or my colander.

The problem is that everything has its place at our house, but certain residents aren't careful about returning things to their proper place.

In fact, I'm going to tape this page to the front of the refrigerator ... if I can just find the Scotch tape.

I always choose the wrong line

I always get in the wrong line.

This is something I've known for a long time, but it's just lately that I've been able to accept the fact that for the rest of my life I'll be getting in the wrong line.

I came to this realization last week while waiting for gas. There were two lines to choose from and I had about 30 seconds to make a decision. I chose the left line. I don't know why I chose the left line, but after only two minutes I realized I had made a mistake. By then it was too late. The other line was moving ahead rapidly and I was stuck.

So while I waited in line I had plenty of time to reflect on my life, and that's when it hit me that fate had destined me to be in the wrong line for the rest of my days.

The supermarket is a good example. When it's time to check out, I always scrutinize the situation and choose the shortest line. But it always backfires. Invariably the woman in front of me has a can of peas that doesn't have a price mark on it, and the checkout person has to call a stock boy to go back to the peas section and find out what the price of one can is.

On the rare occasion that doesn't happen, there will be a person in front of me in line who has to cash a check. And we all know what that means. First the customer has to ask for a pen, and then the correct date. After the check is presented, the customer has to provide a driver's license number, Social Security number, color of eyes, height, employment, five telephone numbers, seven credit references, ten items of identification, etc. After that lengthy procedure, a special call goes out for the manager to come and OK the check. It almost always takes five minutes.

I'm usually the one right behind that customer, fuming while my ice cream melts and my kids grab packs of gum from the checkout counter and tear magazine covers from the nearby rack.

Occasionally I will qualify for the "eight items or less" line. But when I do make it under the limit, I'm always behind a customer with 20 items or more.

The supermarket isn't the only place I get caught in the wrong line. The bank where I keep what little money I've got has a choice of no less than ten drive-in bank windows. What a decision it is for me! I get sweaty palms as I turn the steering wheel from one direction to another.

I carefully study each line, counting cars and the number of occupants in each car. I've learned that two adults in one car sometimes take longer because there are twice as many transactions. And if there is a van in one line, it makes the line appear longer than it is. And if there is a car full of children, the bank teller usually takes time to hand out lots of lollypops, which takes extra minutes because the kids often want to trade them in for a different flavor.

No matter how much thought and deliberation go into my selection, I always end up in the line that moves the slowest. The driver in front of me usually has three checks to cash, one check to deposit, and five withdrawals to make from four separate savings accounts. Or I often get stuck behind a driver who wants to pay the electric bill, the phone bill, the water bill, the rubbish pickup bill, the cable TV bill and the car loan, each with separate checks and separate receipts, and each taking a good two minutes.

It's a lucky thing my car has air conditioning, because I get pretty hot under the collar when this type of thing happens, and it almost always does. When I get so mad that I switch lines, the line I was in usually clears right through and the new line usually blocks up behind some man whose account doesn't balance and he wants to know why. I can't seem to win.

I only have to face the lines at the auto inspection station once a year, but each year I seem to make the wrong choice. With four lines to select from, I try to get in the line with the biggest trucks. With my twisted logic I always assume such a line with four cars and three long trucks will move faster than a line with nine cars, even though both lines are equal in length. I'm always wrong. The line I get in always has some vehicle that fails the brake test and has to back up and try it again. Or a slow inspector. Or a driver who doesn't understand the inspection.

When I'm shopping at one of those large discount stores that have several checkout counters, I usually end up in back of a customer who has to pay with a check, who has a toy to return and wants cash, not credit. That alone is good for a five-minute argument, and at that point I usually move to another line. I find it best to avoid those messy arguments.

Those were my thoughts while waiting in line for gasoline. And as I waited behind four cars filling up completely empty tanks, I watched the drivers in the other line top off with only a few gallons each and head on their way. If I'd only been in the other line, I would have been home by now, I thought to myself.

Just one of those days

Did you ever have one of those days where absolutely nothing goes right?

I woke up one day last week to a beautiful sunny day and was so inspired by it that I thought I'd get up, get all my work done and treat myself to a day at the beach.

I threw my kingsize bedspread into the washer and proceeded to start on my ironing. I was on my second or third pillow case and realized something was wrong. Instead of gliding over the cloth, my iron was acting as though it were pressing a piece of flypaper. Oh no, I thought, not another new iron gone to pot. Then I glanced down at the spray "starch" I had been using -- a brand new can of Shout spot remover!

As I stood there calling myself about every name in the book for being so dumb I smelled something burning. It was smoke coming from the washer. The bedspread had become so heavy when wet that it broke the machine when it tried to spin it dry. Just great.

I picked up the phone to call the appliance store.

"Our service department line is busy right now. Can you hold?"

Sixty seconds later I'm still on hold. They should be getting back to me any second.

Two minutes later and still holding. This is ridiculous. I haven't got all day. I'll give them one more minute then I'll hang up.

It's been two more minutes and they still didn't answer. Just like the dryer, now I'm really burned up. Maybe I've been cut off. Shall I hang up and call again? How long do you wait on hold before you know you've been cut off?

Well, to heck with everything, I said to myself. I'm going to forget the rest of the housework today and head for the beach. At least there I can relax and nothing can go wrong. Right?

Wrong! I never stopped to think about the traffic!

What a shock. The traffic to the beach was bumper to bumper. I waited. And I waited. And I waited. My baby was screaming from being cooped up in the car seat for so long and by that time yours truly was desperately hunting for a bathroom. The sky was clouding up, the clock was moving ahead and I still hadn't reached my destination. By this time I, too, was crying.

We did get to spend a half hour at the beach but by then the traffic was so heavy that I had to start back so I could pick up my other daughter at school. We inched our way back toward Fort Myers and I prayed constantly that I wouldn't run out of gas.

Once home I decided to make a good dinner to cheer myself up. I had spent well over an hour whipping up a fancy French dish when I reached into the spice cabinet to get the pepper. Well, my hand accidently hit the glass jar of garlic salt. The jar fell from the cabinet, landed on the rim of the mixing bowl and shattered into a million tiny pieces - - all over my dinner!

I could have died. I cleaned up the mess, got a pack of hot dogs out of the freezer and went to bed.

The next thing I knew my husband was home standing at the foot of the bed shaking his head in mock disapproval. He stood there with a big smile on his face saying, "Boy, oh

"Oh, God, not another beautiful day!"

boy. I work hard all day and when I come home I find you
laying in bed taking it easy!"
    The pillow that I threw at him bent his glasses!

11

Love is where you find it

Congratulations!
You made it through another year

This coming Valentine's Day millions of married couples all over the world can celebrate the fact that they made it through another year.

Yes, all you couples who still consider yourselves sweethearts should be mighty proud of the fact that you've been able to overlook the little things like overflowing garbage cans, dirty dishes in the sink, hassles over report cards and morning breath that stinks!

It's the little things that can sometimes drive a marriage over the brink. Do you know what I mean?

Come on, girls. How many of you have gotten up to go to the bathroom in the middle of the night only to fall right into the bowl because the toilet seat was left up?

Or how many of you men spend hour after hour cleaning the family car only to have the wife and kids treat it like a movable garbage can?

Sound familiar?

They say opposites attract. It must be true because with most couples I know there is one person who likes to grab a tube of toothpaste and squeeze it with gay abandon married to another who insists on rolling up the tube neatly with great deliberation.

And the sheets and blankets at night! Why is it that whenever you're hot he's cold and then when you finally do cool off and reach for the blankets they're gone because he's taken them all?

In our house the heater and air-conditioner go up and down like the tide. It's funny because neither of us says a word to each other but whenever we go over to adjust the thermostat it is never where we left it. It must be a ghost!

114

The poor men must shudder at times when they think back on the beautiful bride they married as she sits across the breakfast table now, hair in rollers, makeup smeared, and wrapped up in an old holey nightie.

But on the other hand a receding hairline and little beer belly is not always a joy to behold in the morning either.

And why is it that men are willing to share almost everything with their wives except their electric razors? They can shave their faces with it every day and that's okay. But try to borrow it just once to shave your legs and watch out! You'd think you were asking to borrow the crown jewels!

Another funny thing about husbands is how they hate to ask for directions when they're traveling. I'm beginning to think it's an inborn male characteristic. No matter how lost they are, they're willing to risk the ridicule and inconvenience of driving a half hour in the wrong direction rather than admit defeat and stop and ask someone which way to go.

Of course, some women are not an all-out joy to travel with either. Some of us just have weak kidneys and many of us managed to go all through high school or college without ever learning how to read a map. And while we spend all day in the car at home carting kids between school, music lessons and soccer practice, when trip time comes we suddenly forget how and somehow manage to make the poor man do most of the driving.

But I think the couples that deserve the most credit for staying together are those which include one partner who is **ALWAYS RIGHT**. Or even worse, one who just thinks he's always right.

And I won't even go into the snoring, the pre-dawn operas in the shower and the insistance on asking the correct time instead of wearing a watch. Suffice it to say, they can drive you bats!

But somehow -- miraculously -- many married couples manage to overlook each other's shortcomings and grow closer and closer as the years go by. They are still each other's Valentines and isn't that what love is all about?

Oh, for a lost weekend!

My daughter sauntered up to me recently and asked what I wanted for Mother's Day.

"Three days at a hotel -- alone!" I shot back without a moment's hesitation.

I think she was a little taken aback. She had been expecting me to say something more conventional, I'm sure. Something like "a nice little tin can, painted with red and yellow flowers, with a lid on it so I will have some place to keep my jewelry." Or maybe "a big bottle of that sweet-smelling perfume that you can buy in the drug store." Or perhaps "a lovely necklace made of string and broken seashells."

But I decided it was important to prepare her for real life. She'll be a mother some day herself, and she better know right from the start that it's no bed of roses.

"Oh, I get it," she said with a little smile. "You want us all to go on a vacation, right?"

Wrong, I told her. I guess the idea of a vacation for mother is too remote to even conjecture.

"Where do you want to go?" she asked.

That's a tough one to explain. Right now I'd settle for three days alone anywhere but my own house.

"Why would you want to spend three days by yourself?" she asked. I just laughed.

Well, for one thing there wouldn't be any dirty dishes to worry about, I told her. Dirty dishes have a way of traveling all over our home. They're in the bedrooms, the bathrooms, the closets, under tables and behind chairs. They're everywhere, in fact, except the dishwasher.

And then there's the laundry. Washing the clothes isn't so bad, although it's beyond me why little girls have to wear so many different outfits a day. It's folding the clean laundry that I want to avoid. Sorting socks, folding underpants, hanging up shirts so they won't wrinkle -- there would be none of that at my three-day getaway.

And of course there's the cooking. Three meals a day,

seven days a week, doesn't even begin to tell the story at our house. There are mid-morning snacks and late-night desserts and everything in between. At the hotel, I wouldn't have to worry about what's for dinner.

I wouldn't have to be the family chauffeur, either, if I were spending three days at a hotel -- alone. No trips to the store, no trips to the school, no trips to the bank, no trips to the post office, no trips to the doctor's office, no trips at all.

"But what would you do for three days all by yourself?" she asked.

Oh, it makes me tremble just to imagine.

The first day I think I would just lie in bed and read -- I've got dozens of magazines that I haven't finished, and hundreds of books that I haven't started. But I wouldn't read a single children's book.

When I got hungry, I would call room service and have them deliver something special. I would turn on the radio and listen to soft music as I ate. Or maybe I would just eat in silence. Yes, that's it. I would eat in total silence. Wow! This is getting better!

Then after dinner I would call room service and have someone take my tray away. No dirty dishes to clean, no dirty hands to wipe, no dirty high chair to scrub, no dirty carpet to vacuum.

I would stay up and watch the late show on television, and I would sleep until at least noon the next day. After a leisurely lunch, I would do something special.

If my hotel were at the beach, I would walk along by myself, picking up seashells and watching the birds. I wouldn't have to watch the kids battle the waves in six inches of water. I might even take a book to the beach and read it. That would be a real treat.

If my hotel were in the city, I would shop in the stores all afternoon -- by myself. I wouldn't have to worry about the kids knocking down a display case of china. I wouldn't have to worry about the sales clerks talking about my girls behind my back. I wouldn't have to worry about keeping the kids entertained while at the same time trying to squeeze into a new swimsuit in the dressing room.

After I went to the beach or on the shopping spree, I

would stop at an ice cream store and buy a cone just for myself. I wouldn't have to share it with anyone.

While I was out of the hotel room, a maid would have made the bed and cleaned the room. There would be no toothpaste in the sink, no towels on the floor, no soap in the tub. It sounds so nice, I think I would probably take a leisurely bath. There would be no little hands knocking on the door and screaming to "let me in!"

"But wouldn't that be lonely?" my daughter asked, bursting her way into my daydream.

No, I wouldn't be lonely. At least not for the first five minutes. But then I would go into the bathroom and check to see if the toilet paper roll was empty. And I would wash the sanitized plastic glasses. And I would wonder if the telephone was broken since it wasn't ringing. And then I would be convinced the kids were up to something because of the deafening silence.

I probably wouldn't last one afternoon of my three-day getaway. But it's nice to think about.

Star struck

I wonder what I'll get for Mother's Day this year -- a Star Wars poster, a can of Slime, or a Shaun Cassidy T-shirt?

Or maybe, Heaven forbid, I'll get some of that awful new Space Dust that you sprinkle into your mouth and it sizzles like mad on your tongue.

But believe it or not, I can't wait.

Mother's Day has got to be one of my favorite days of the year 'cause that's when my husband takes my little girl shopping with piggy bank in hand and lets her choose the one perfect gift she feels I simply can't do without. There's a lot of thought and love that goes into the choosing of these presents and I can't help being thrilled with them.

My 8-year-old has been on a star kick for about two years now. That phase started several Christmases ago when she bought me what has to be her all time favorite -- a big rhinestone star pin for $1.35 that she said reminded her of "the star over Bethlehem." Oh, she was so proud of that pin. So proud, in fact, that she wanted and expected me to wear it everywhere I went, be it to the grocery store or to a formal dance.

One day several weeks later I forgot to take it off the shirt before doing the laundry and when I took it out it looked like a piece of decorative swiss cheese. Half of the "beautiful jewels" were missing!

Panic stricken, I hopped in the car while she was at nursery school and made a bee line to the five and ten cent store. I quickly told the salesperson my tale of woe and after a thorough search we found one left, on sale, for 50 cents. At that point, I think I would have paid anything for it. At any rate, I wore it that night at the dinner table. I knew my efforts were well worth it when she suddenly announced, "Mother, you look beautiful tonight."

Last Mother's Day it was a necklace. It was a "silver" chain with a red, a white and a blue star in the middle of it. Unfortunately, I was allergic to the metal this gem was made of, but I was able to wear it once or twice for the effect.

This Christmas she had finally decided on a Star Wars poster when she happened upon a Christmas ornament shaped like a star and covered with silver sparkles. Well, she fell completely in love with it.

"Isn't it beautiful?" she exclaimed as she helped me open it on Christmas Day. When I looked at it through her eyes, it truly was.

But this year for Mother's Day I don't know. She's been hinting around a lot about some Shaun Cassidy T-shirt. Or maybe she'll start on the kind of gifts I used to give when I was a kid - pictures, pot holders and perfume.

Why, I'd buy purple perfume, green perfume and yellow perfume. Any kind, in fact, so long as it was pretty and smelly (oh, was it ever) and came in a big, beautiful bottle.

But whatever the gifts happen to be I know I'll cherish them for years to come because of the love that went into them. I've been blessed with two beautiful, healthy and loving daughters and to me that's the greatest gift of all.

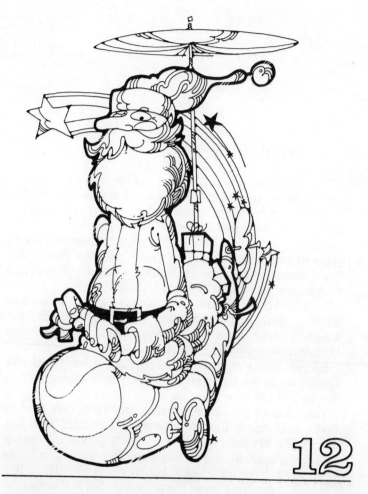

12

Where is Santa
when you need him?

Glad tidings

Christmas isn't the best time of year to be in Florida.

First of all, there's no snow. And no matter how low the temperature on our thermometer dips (maybe 45 degrees at worst) cold weather is no substitute for snow.

I know I'm going to hear a lot of snide comments from all you sun lovers! But be honest. Don't you get a pang in the heart when you hear the jingle bells of Santa's helpers and then see Santa step out in shorts and sandals?

I'll admit that Christmas shopping is a lot easier without all that slush and those heavy coats and mittens. But wouldn't some snow on the windowsills brighten your Christmas morning?

I keep telling everybody that it just doesn't feel like Christmas in the sunshine. And everybody glares back at me, as if to say "are you crazy?"

Then there's the Christmas tree. Have you ever tried to find a real tree in Florida over seven feet tall? They just don't exist. My theory is that some nasty person is stopping all the trucks in North Carolina and pulling off any Christmas tree that looks halfway decent. Then this Scrooge is marking up all the price tags 200 percent on the trees that are left, and sending the trucks on their way to Florida.

The final blow came this year. Christmas cards became nearly non-existent. I figure someone in the post office was lonely and kept all the Christmas cards addressed to me for himself. Either that, or the price of cards and postage has gotten so high that my friends can't afford to send Christmas cards anymore.

I remember back in the good old days when it cost 5 cents for a stamp, the Christmas cards flowed freely. Even our insurance agent sent us a card. But now he must be feeling the effects of inflation like everyone else.

I must admit, I wasn't too surprised when we only received a few cards this year. I stopped sending them last year, and I guess in the true holiday spirit, if you don't send cards to your friends, they stop sending cards to you. My theory is that if Hallmark Cards doesn't buy out the post office and lower the postage rates, sooner or later Hallmark is going to go bust. And if that happens, the government will take away the holidays.

I don't miss the cards so much, but what I do miss are all those mimeographed letters that I used to get at Christmas time. Without those letters, I just don't know all the family achievements of my long-lost friends.

Take my old school friend Joanne, for instance. The last time I heard from Joanne, her little boy was named to "Who's Who in Primary Schools." And her husband had just been promoted to "a very important post with a very prominent bank." Joanne, of course, was "constantly busy because of her involvement in charity work and her position in the Junior League." Her dog was "best of show at the Grosse Pointe dog show," and their vacation cruise to the Mediterranean "was simply elegant." To top it off, she enclosed a newspaper clipping about her "fantastic talent in needle point" and the one-woman show she presented the previous summer.

A few letters like that make my own life seem pretty bland. I've always wanted to send out those Christmas letters to my friends, but I've never really had anything very interesting to write about. Who cares that my youngest daughter is finally potty-trained, or that my oldest daughter finally learned how to make her own bed. Our vacation this year was a weekend on Sanibel -- a rainy weekend at that. My biggest achievement was putting 10,000 miles on our car driving back and forth to the store, school and home. The only time I was featured in the paper this year was when my advertisement for my garage sale appeared in The Shopper.

Somehow my life doesn't lend itself to one of those Christmas letters. But now I have a better excuse for not sending them -- the price of stamps is just too high!

Make mine gold

Dear Santa,

Please don't leave a food processor under my Christmas tree this year, no matter how great the temptation.

If you want to put a gold bracelet under the tree, that would be great. A nice new frilly dress would be fine. Diamond earrings or Gucci shoes would make me happy. But please don't bring me something for the kitchen.

I know that a lot of women want one of those new convection ovens, and I would like to have one, too. But not for Christmas! That's one morning I don't want to have to think about cooking, cleaning and dirty dishes.

I realize that a food processor would save me time in the kitchen, and I could dream up hundreds of new and interesting ways to serve chicken. But for Christmas I want something for myself.

I saw my husband head toward the housewares section last week with a gleam in his eye. The first thing he stopped at was an electric pasta machine, guaranteed to turn out homemade pasta paper thin. Just what I need! I'm on a diet.

The next thing that caught his eye was an espresso coffee machine that makes exotic-sounding coffee at the flip of a switch. In my house it would just be one more thing to dust.

It didn't take long for him to notice a beautiful woman demonstrating the hottest thing in kitchen gadgets this year -- the convection oven. He watched as the woman pulled a beautifully brown cornish hen out of the oven and he listened to her sales pitch about how the convection oven continuously circulates hot air to cook food evenly and cheaply. As he heard the word "cheaply," his eyes lit up.

When he saw the price tag, his eyes opened wider and he turned to the next counter.

That's when he noticed the food processor. Now deep down in his heart my husband always wanted me to have a food processor. "It would make it so easy for you to fix all those special meals," he once told me. Personally, I don't think a food processor would be as helpful as a gadget that could cook chicken in 100 different and tasty new ways.

A lot of my friends have food processors, and they use them about as often as they use their silver-plated duck shears. And frankly, my kitchen is crowded enough without a food processor.

I don't know why men think it's fun for women to get kitchen gadgets as gifts. We spend half our lives in the kitchen, and on Christmas morning I personally would like to forget about cooking. To me, it's about as exciting as opening up a pretty present and discovering an iron inside.

Two or three years ago my husband presented me with an electric cookie, canape and candy maker. He thought it was a great gift. Actually, it's never been used.

So Santa, if you have any influence at all, please persuade my husband against a food processor. Ditto for a pressure cooker, a set of German stainless steel knives with ebony handles, a solid maple butcher block, a matched set of copper cookware, or even a microwave oven.

A simple gift of gold or silver will do nicely, thank you. And I don't mean silver plated tableware. I want something for me, this year, not for the family.

And if you come through for me, Santa, I promise not to give my husband a box of trash bags or a case of chlorine for the pool as his Christmas gift. I have a feeling he wouldn't appreciate seeing a new battery for his car under the tree on Christmas morning.

Hope to see you on Christmas eve. I'll be the one in an apron with the words "cook it yourself" in big red letters.

Love,
DEBBY

Off to the same old start

Don't you just hate making New Year's resolutions?
After all, it's one thing to sit down and search your soul
for ways to improve yourself. But to have the deter-
mination and endurance to carry them out, well, that's a
different matter.

This year I decided to avoid all those sweet and well-
meaning general resolutions like keeping my temper with
the children and being more loving to my husband.
They're okay for a week or so, but after that they're long
forgotten.

Nope. This year I'm going to take the old bull by the
horns and make some specific resolutions that I'm more
likely to carry out.

For example:

• Take down the Christmas tree by the first of February ...
at least by the first of March ... well definitely by April 1.

• Pack the Christmas tree lights neatly so I don't have to
spend three hours untangling them next year.

• Start ironing my husband's shirts. But first, I've just got
to find the iron.

• Buy myself new underwear and throw out all the ones
that resemble swiss cheese. It might be a good idea to do
the same with my husband's socks.

• Try to figure out my way around Cape Coral.

• Throw away all the left-over Halloween candy by
Valentine's Day.

• Empty the diaper pail every other day, whether it needs
it or not.

• Stop eating Christmas cookies and candy at midnight
Dec. 31 ... or stop kidding myself about this the first of
every year.

• Start buying Christmas presents early for next
Christmas. The traffic is too bad on Dec. 24.

• Buy a pencil sharpener. Sixty-two pencils that don't
write is too much for any house.

• Start an organized file of the hundreds of recipes I've

clipped over the past 10 years. Toss out the hundreds I've never tried.

•Clean off the Kool-Aid from the refrigerator shelves. They are just too sticky.

•Keep check stubs.

•Be prompt in writing thank you notes.(Who am I kidding?)

•Throw out all the cartoon jelly glasses I have accumulated and buy eight matching glasses.

• Learn how to uncurdle Hollandaise sauce.

• Stop saving all the magazines I never have time to read. Things aren't getting any better!

•Remember to stop throwing artichokes down the garbage disposal. These plumbing bills are just getting out of hand.

•Stop making New Year's resolutions!

Another Copy?

Wouldn't you love to have a copy of this book to send to your relatives up North, or your mother-in-law across the state, or your friends across the street?

Well, through the magic of the U.S. Postal Service, and a little luck, "Oh, God, not another beautiful day!" can put a little sunshine in their lives, too. All it takes is your check or money order for $5.95 per copy or three books for $15, plus 80 cents postage and handling for each book ordered. (Florida residents, add 5 percent sales tax. That's 30 cents per book.)

If you want me to send the book directly to your friends or relatives, please print their name, address and zip code legibly on a piece of paper and send it along with your order. Jot down your phone number, too, in case I have a question.

Send your order to: Debby Wood, Box 1737, Cape Coral, FL 33910.

"Oh, God, not another beautiful day!"

Please send me _____ copies . . . . $ _____
    1 copy is $5.95
    Three copies for $15.00

Florida residents add 5% sales tax . . . . . . $ _____
    30 cents per book

Add shipping . . . . $ _____
    80 cents per book

                                TOTAL $ _____

NAME _____

ADDRESS_____

CITY/STATE/ZIP _____

PHONE NUMBER _____

Make checks payable to Debby Wood
Mail to: Debby Wood, Box 1737, Cape Coral, FL 33910